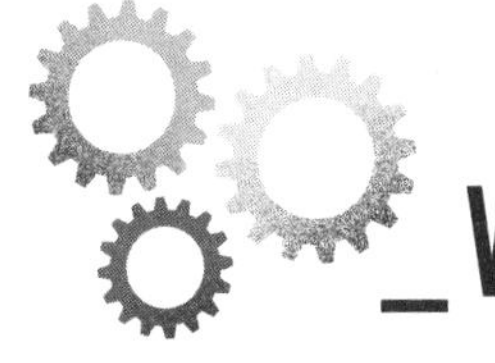

WHEN WORKING TOGETHER DOESN'T WORK

Foreword by
SUZANNE STABILE

AN ENNEAGRAM GUIDE *to* PRODUCTIVE RELATIONSHIPS *with* COWORKERS

JOEY STABILE SCHEWEE

An imprint of InterVarsity Press
Downers Grove, Illinois

InterVarsity Press
P.O. Box 1400 | Downers Grove, IL 60515-1426
ivpress.com | email@ivpress.com

InterVarsity Press® is the publishing division of InterVarsity Christian Fellowship/USA®. For more information, visit intervarsity.org.

While any stories in this book are true, some names and identifying information may have been changed to protect the privacy of individuals.

The publisher cannot verify the accuracy or functionality of website URLs used in this book beyond the date of publication.

Cover design: Faceout Studio
Interior design: Daniel van Loon
Cover images: © jozefmicic via Adobe Stock
Interior images: InterVarsity Press

ISBN 978-1-5140-1162-1 (print) | ISBN 978-1-5140-1163-8 (digital)

Printed in the United States of America ♾

Library of Congress Cataloging-in-Publication Data
A catalog record for this book is available from the Library of Congress.

33 32 31 30 29 28 27 26 | 12 11 10 9 8 7 6 5 4 3 2 1

"Joey Stabile Schewee masterfully accomplishes what few have been able to. She guides her audiences toward practical application of the Enneagram in secular spaces while honoring both the integrity of this wisdom and the reality of the human experience in today's world."
Richard Rohr, founder of the Center for Action and Contemplation

"People often ask me to recommend a good, concise introduction to the Enneagram, and while there are a few around, none are better than Joey Schewee's *When Working Together Doesn't Work.* This book is clear, to the point, and hugely practical in how it explains how the self-knowledge the Enneagram provides can help us better navigate the ups and downs of relationships and professional challenges. Joey includes all the significant teachings of the Enneagram without getting lost in the details and delivers a fantastic entry into a way of knowing yourself that can serve you the rest of your life. Highly recommended."
Russ Hudson, coauthor with Don Richard Riso of *The Wisdom of the Enneagram* and author of *The Enneagram: Nine Gateways to Presence*

"A practical guide to workplace dynamics through the Enneagram lens. Joey Schewee's key insight: We can't change our motivation (how we see the world), but we can change our behavior (what we do). She explores the Centers of Intelligence—Doing, Feeling, and Thinking—showing how colleagues approach tasks differently, creating conflict without malice. By encouraging balance across these centers, the book provides a framework for resilient teams and healthier collaboration. Essential reading for leaders seeking to transform workplace tension into understanding."
Sharon K. Ball, founder of 9Paths and author of *Reclaiming You: Using the Enneagram to Move from Trauma to Resilience*

"*When Working Together Doesn't Work* isn't just another personality book; it's a practical guide to understanding motivation, easing tension, and pursuing shared goals with integrity. Joey Schewee makes the Enneagram simple and actionable, offering insight you can apply right away. Whether you're leading a team, collaborating with coworkers, or navigating workplace challenges, this book equips you to communicate clearly, handle conflict wisely, and draw out the best in every type."
Brittany Thomas, founder of enneagramexplained.com

"*When Working Together Doesn't Work* is a game-changer for teams seeking deeper understanding and more effective collaboration. With practical, Enneagram-based strategies tailored to each personality type, both for managing and being managed, this book offers a road map to navigating workplace dynamics with empathy and insight. Our team is already seeing the benefits of clearer communication and mutual respect. A must-read for anyone serious about building productive relationships at work."
Betsy Stein, healthcare administrator

"In this highly readable and uncommonly practical book, Joey Stabile Schewee not only guides readers in understanding the Enneagram, but she also uniquely applies it to the relationships found in the place we spend many of our waking hours—our work environment. Applied properly, the reading of *When Working Together Doesn't Work* will help you improve the quality and durability of relationships and the performance of your teams."

Jeff Crosby, author of *The Language of the Soul* and *World of Wonders*

For Billy

You always bring out the best in me because you see the best in me.

Thank you for being my greatest advocate.

For Will and Sam

Being your mother is fulfilling in every possible way.

Thank you for giving me the most rewarding job of all.

For my trailblazing mother

It is an honor to follow in your footsteps.

Thank you for teaching me that there is strength in vulnerability.

For my father

Your wisdom and discernment have shaped my life.

Thank you for being our guide.

CONTENTS

FOREWORD

Suzanne Stabile

JOEY AND I BEGAN LEARNING the Enneagram at the same time. She was enjoying her last year as a teenager, and I was in the process of finding my place in midlife. We were on a family vacation headed to Colorado and while we made that two-day trip every year, it was the first time we did so with a boyfriend in the car.

I had imagined what it might be like for Billy to be in the car with our family of six for the 830-mile trip. Entertainment of some kind seemed essential, and I had just purchased a cassette series recorded by Helen Palmer describing the nine numbers of the Enneagram. I thought, *You can't go wrong with that*, and I was right. By the time we arrived in Lake City my husband, Joe, and I, and our daughters Jenny and Joey, knew our numbers, and Billy seemed to be sure of his. That trip was the beginning of an unexpected journey for all of us in relation to Enneagram wisdom.

In the three decades since Father Richard Rohr introduced me to the Enneagram, I have built a successful career teaching and writing about it. During these years I've discovered that there is a great need for Enneagram wisdom in corporate America. C-suite executives and other corporate professionals consistently tell me that managing people is the most challenging and time-consuming part of their jobs.

As Joey stepped into midlife she courageously left her job as chief advancement officer of a large private school to work full time teaching the

Enneagram. She had a myriad of opportunities to use the Enneagram while consulting in professional environments. She has enough experience to know that as human beings we have a lot to learn about one another, and there is value in allowing and naming difference rather than trying to tame it. Joey is super smart, very strong, and kind. Those attributes along with her life experience have helped pave the way for her to make a significant contribution to a growing body of Enneagram wisdom that holds true to traditional teaching while offering new and creative ways for responding to life in the twenty-first century.

Joey is a master in her use and application of this ancient wisdom. Enneagram wisdom has a form of its own language. Those who speak and understand it well can teach it efficiently and effectively, and those who don't cannot. The primary thing that separates Joey's work from others is that while she is fluent in "Enneaspeak," she uses her own dialect to teach in professional settings. Essentially, she has adapted the wisdom and the vocabulary so that both speak directly to the unique challenges associated with professional environments and work.

The reality of living in a postmodern society is that we have more questions than answers, and more problems than solutions. The problem-solving mechanisms that once worked no longer do, and people are more polarized than at any time in recent history. If we are going to take more steps forward than backward, we will need a map that shows us the way without unnecessary detours and distractions.

You can't change what you can't name. In the book you are holding in your hand, Joey teaches you how to see life through the lens of the Enneagram. In seeing this way, using words you already know but in the way she uses them, you will have the potential to name and address all that needs your attention in a non-personal and therefore non-threatening way. As I see the world, that is the only way to work with other people, offering them both dignity and respect. It is also our best hope for building the kind of communities we all want to belong to.

In the pages that follow you will find out why you continue to do the very things you don't want to do. You will read about people who drive you crazy and hopefully understand why. You might even consider the possibility that you drive them crazy too. You will have the opportunity to understand why it will not be helpful if you continue to hire people who are just like you. You can take another look at how you are viewed by the people who may report to you. There are tips for managing others and there is so much more.

Once you know the Enneagram you can't un-know it! That has been true for our family plus one boyfriend since we drove over Slumgullion Pass leading into Lake City, Colorado, almost thirty years ago. In case you are wondering, Joey married Billy, and they have two sons. The Enneagram has informed how they care for their marriage and how they are raising Will and Sam. They both have used it extensively in their professional lives, and they teach an Enneagram Cohort for Life in the Trinity Ministry. In addition, they have developed a model for teaching the Enneagram and parenting.

Joey teaches all over the country—sometimes in corporate America, and at other times in colleges and universities, churches, nonprofit organizations, and any other place where people are partnering with one another hoping to affect the world in a positive way.

It is a joy for her daddy, Rev. Joseph Stabile, and me to have the honor of being her parents. And it is a privilege for me to have been asked to write the foreword for this book.

INTRODUCTION

WHEN IT COMES TO WORKING WELL with others, self-knowledge is a crucial first step. Our capacity for understanding others correlates to our ability to self-reflect, and nothing promotes candid self-reflection quite like the Enneagram. Those who are intentional about utilizing this tool for individual transformation discover manifold benefits, both personal and professional. The principal reason why pairing this wisdom with a spiritual journey consistently proves to be effective is that the Enneagram honors the remarkable uniqueness of the individual human experience.

Consider a company president who is experiencing mounting tensions with his company's CFO. The CFO is a tenured employee who conscientiously devoted his career to the company and has openly struggled in recent years to align himself with the strategic vision of the president and a younger COO. Applying an Enneagram lens to this dynamic equips the president first and foremost with a realistic view of his own core motivation prior to shifting his focus to the CFO and the rest of his executive team.

Utilizing the Enneagram, the president knows that his motivation is grounded in feeling (as opposed to thinking or doing) while the CFO's motivation is grounded in doing (as opposed to thinking or feeling). Their continued misalignment threatens both a valued relationship (a priority for the president) and an effective chain of command (a priority for the CFO). Without this motivational awareness, scapegoating would inevitably lead to dissolution of the relationship, the chain of command, and the overall efficacy of the business. By contrast,

Enneagram understanding removes personal slights and fosters relational objectivity, restoring a crucial element easily discarded in the face of disagreement: sincere intentions.

Nine Ways of Seeing

One would be hard-pressed to find a functioning society that does not consider a cornerstone of prosocial behavior to be treating others as one wants to be treated. The Golden Rule or Ethic of Reciprocity is a fundamental social norm that surfaces in global culture across history. What if acknowledging the fallibility of this rule was a prerequisite to achieving the heightened social awareness that the rule universally promises? What if the most constructive way to "love thy neighbor" is to acknowledge and allow a perspective that is different from thine own?

Take me, for example. What I want from others is direct, blunt honesty. If you mince your words or withhold details to spare my feelings, I do not respond well. So, from a young age, I offered blunt honesty to those around me. Family, friends, and coworkers knew to come to me if they wanted a direct answer. Those who stayed around me long enough to get to know me appreciated that I would "tell it like it is." While it bolstered my altruistic intentions, the Ethic of Reciprocity insulated me from facing the reality that most people do not want direct bluntness, nor do they appreciate it.

As I approach forty-seven years and the second half of life, I look back on my adulthood with deep gratitude for the wisdom of a tool that I was exposed to at that pristine moment in life when my personal lens superseded all others: my final year as a teenager. My journey of self-discovery and, equally important, the discovery that there are unique ways of seeing and approaching every situation life presents us, has been transformative. Transformation is by no means simple or easy. While three decades of employing Enneagram wisdom did not insulate me from poignant life lessons, it has been a natural compass and powerful touchstone guiding my understanding that the way I approach the world is not the same for others.

So, what makes this compass so powerful? In my estimation, the Enneagram is singular in its effectiveness at fostering self-examination, first, and promoting understanding and compassion for others, second. Within the vast industry of personality typing systems, the Enneagram continues to exist in a category all its own as the only system to type on motivation as opposed to behavior. In Enneagram understanding, there are nine unique motivations that inform human behavior.

My consistent response to those who might label this system reductive (how can there *only* be nine motivations) is to acknowledge the reality of human agency. There are billions of iterations of human behavior, yet the motivations that inform those behaviors can be traced to nine ways of seeing. Our behaviors adjust and evolve based on any number of internal and external factors, yet the way we see—our intrinsic motivation—is elemental and does not change. In other words, we cannot alter how we see (motivation), but we can alter what we do with how we see (behavior). The aptitude that rises from applying motivational understanding within a work environment does not surface in predicting what employees will do—human agency will invariably supplant that—but in grasping why employees do what they do.

As a management consultant and executive coach who has built a practice entirely from employing the Enneagram in professional environments, 70 percent of my clients are long-term. I believe this speaks directly to the limitless application of this tool and the reality that it does not contradict but rather enhances existing systems while bridging generational divides. These clients have woven the Enneagram seamlessly into five-generation cultures that were built favoring systems like MBTI, DiSC, Clifton Strengths, and Big Five.

There is a nondualism aspect to the Enneagram that this English major and Business minor, right and left brained, nerdy athlete, rebel preacher's daughter finds refreshing. It is believed to be drawn from Eastern and Western philosophies and, while it very neatly fits into categories that favor subjective interpretation, I have always found its teachings to make substantial logical sense. So, to be blunt, let's dive in.

Part I

HOW THE ENNEAGRAM WORKS

When Working Together Doesn't Work is not a lengthy read. As an Enneagram Eight who values efficiency and effectiveness, you will hopefully discern my intention to present a tool that carries profound wisdom with meaningful brevity. Whether you have existing knowledge of this system or this is your first exposure, the Enneagram is comprised of numerous moving parts that may seem daunting to grasp initially. In an effort to shorten the learning curve, Part I will include optional reflection questions placed in Appendix B. These questions have been thoughtfully designed to prioritize and promote comprehension of the three native intelligence centers and their converging influence on our unique motivations. Even if you skip around the book or read ahead, your intentionality with the first section will undoubtedly correlate to your grasp of the remaining material.

Much like the Enneagram serves as an illuminating accompaniment to other systems that foster self-examination, so too will these questions complement and facilitate your individual understanding, a critical prerequisite to realizing the full benefit of this wisdom. An unexpectedly sizable portion of my consulting work has been devoted to helping people who have mistyped to discover their true Enneagram type. It is likely that one-third of people mistype themselves when learning the Enneagram. This prevalence for mistyping is often attributed to a general misunderstanding surrounding the Centers of Intelligence and their influence on motivation. Mistyping robs you of the tangible benefits that consciously bringing the Centers of Intelligence into balance provides. The reflection questions found in Appendix B can be useful for fostering honest self-examination and illuminating inherent strengths and blind spots that you carry as an individual contributor to your team.

Consider two seasoned CPAs who work for the same accounting firm. Both individuals process with the Thinking Center of Intelligence (as opposed to doing or feeling). Both employees have been promoted to leadership within the firm and share a similar division of responsibilities. While both employees are proficient at their duties as outlined in their analogous job descriptions, each CPA excels in different areas based on unique motivations.

CPA A shifts from thinking to feeling and is particularly gifted at engaging clients and fellow employees. CPA B shifts from thinking to doing and embraces complex issues like international tax laws with knowledgeable ease. If CPA A takes longer to process returns that are more complex, he more than makes up for it in his client-facing capacity. If CPA B is off-putting with a client, she compensates with unparalleled accuracy and efficiency in return processing.

While cursory examination of their behaviors checks the employer box for what a high-functioning CPA should look like on paper, taking a step further to understand their differing motivations shifts the conversation from a one-size-fits-all job description mentality to an approach that benefits the firm as much as it does the individual CPAs. Shuffling job responsibilities so that CPA A takes the lead on client calls and employee training rejuvenates CPA A, who is starting to feel burned out, and inspires CPA B to spend mental energy and time not squandered on clients researching and developing a thorough FAQ on complex topics for firm associates.

There is a definable limit, especially in the long-term, to the ROI that employers gain from spending time and money analyzing employee behavior. Not so with motivation analysis. When we shift our analysis from *what* to *why*, the depths of understanding that can be achieved are limitless.

CENTERS OF INTELLIGENCE

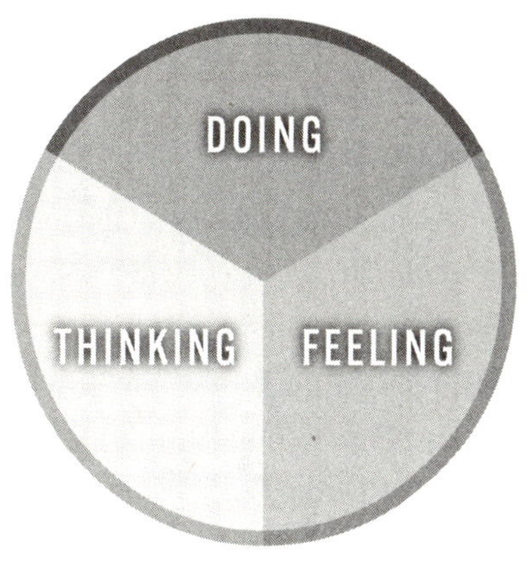

A CRUCIAL ASPECT OF EFFECTIVE SELF-EXAMINATION is to look at *why* we do what we do. Enneagram understanding can be a useful tool in any environment because it provides a road map, of sorts, for navigating the intuitive human motivation that informs observable behaviors. This map is drawn from our three native intelligence centers: the Doing Center, the Feeling Center, and the Thinking Center.

The Centers of Intelligence reference may be Enneagram specific, but the understanding that humans draw from these three centers is not. These centers surface elsewhere in our understanding of human personality and are often identified in the inevitable overlap of philosophy and psychology. Acknowledgment of the interconnectedness of these three centers surfaces in faith and practice for most world religions.

Balance is a key component of historic spiritual enlightenment. In the same way, modern-day application of Enneagram understanding posits that, while we are equipped with all three centers, we do not use them in balance or alignment. Bringing these centers into balance is a principal benefit to using the Enneagram both for self-examination and in our interactions with others.

Once you consider these three centers as equal parts of one whole, layering the Enneagram on top of the centers reveals the intuitive order that we uniquely draw from doing, feeling, and thinking, by Enneagram type.

Doing Center

The Doing Center gives us the motivation to act and implement. It is the center at the top of the Enneagram and is the only center that all nine types are directly connected to with a line. (Twos and Fours have no direct connection to the Thinking Center and Fives and Sevens have no direct connection to the Feeling Center.) In Enneagram language, the Doing Center is also referred to as the Gut Center, reflecting the philosophical convention that gut feeling or intuition represents the interconnectedness of mind, body, and emotions in shaping the human experience.

While the remaining two centers, the Feeling Center and the Thinking Center, can take on any number of interpretations, the Doing Center is more universally understood as the center that equips each of us with the inherent ability to move, to execute, to accomplish, to achieve.

Feeling Center

Moving clockwise around the Enneagram leads to the Feeling or Heart Center. The Feeling Center represents three core elements of the human experience: emotion, people awareness, and subjective thought. These elements continuously converge to make this center inherently interpersonal. Thus, when the Feeling Center is out of balance, our ability to connect with and relate to others suffers.

Mentally working through something does not necessarily mean that you are drawing from the Thinking Center. In Enneagram theory, subjective thought derives wholly from the Feeling Center.

Thinking Center

The third and final Center of Intelligence is the Thinking or Head Center. The Thinking Center equips us with prudence and objective reason, providing the ability to take a step back and observe without allowing emotions to cloud sensible judgment.

An inevitable stumbling block to bringing thinking into balance with feeling and doing is viewing the totality of mental energy as proceeding from the Thinking Center. It can be difficult to acknowledge an imbalance of the Thinking Center when we generally see ourselves as thinking creatures. Rational thought is consistent with facts and reality and is a clear function of the neutral objectivity that the Thinking Center offers.

Lines Matter

Within the Enneagram, we are typed by core motivation, represented as one of nine ways of seeing. Aptly named (*ennea* means nine in Ancient Greek), the Enneagram is a nine-pointed figure that provides a visual for the core motivations and their connection to the Centers of Intelligence. We will dive deeper into the core motivations of each type in the chapters that follow. For now, grasping the importance of lines is prioritized to facilitate conceptual comprehension.

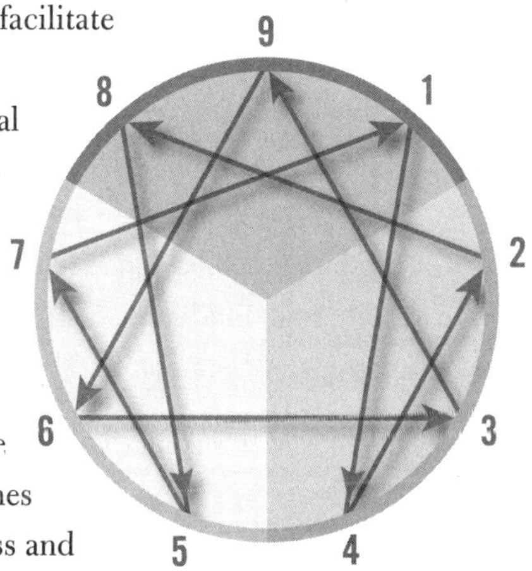

Note, while not nearly as influential as our lines, wings (the numbers on either side of our core type) can influence behavior for some people. Wing influence is outlined in Appendix A.

Stress line and secure line. Each type is connected to two other types via lines that are commonly referred to as stress and security lines. These lines give us unique access to behaviors from other types. The arrow moving away from our core type is known as our stress line because we draw behaviors from the type at the end of that line when we are in stress. Initial exposure to the Enneagram often sparks immediate recognition of core type and stress move because we instinctively utilize the behaviors of our stress move to take care of ourselves. Inherent familiarity with stress-move behaviors can also lead to mistyping if initial exposure happens during a period of personal stress.

Consider an Enneagram Three who initially typed as a Nine months after both of her parents were killed in a tornado, or a Two who typed as an Eight when she learned the Enneagram weeks after being diagnosed with Stage IV breast cancer. Or the Five who identified strongly with Seven when he was exposed to the Enneagram in an attempt to support his son while his daughter-in-law was recovering from a horrific car accident that left her permanently disabled. Stress is so ingrained in the human experience that our intuitive recognition of our stress behaviors can be as strong as our acknowledgment of core motivation.

The arrow pointing toward our core type is known as our secure line because we draw behaviors from the type at the end of that line when we are in a secure space. To be clear, secure does not mean confident, but comfortably vulnerable. The most confident types on the Enneagram are motivated to avoid vulnerability at all costs. Truthfully, it is rare for any of us to navigate life in prolonged states of comfortable vulnerability, so secure behaviors tend to be met with much less cognizance. Whether stress or secure, the moves we make to draw from other types are limited to behavior. Motivation or "hardwiring" is intrinsically tied to core type and is not altered by stress or security.

Stress moves are not inherently bad and secure moves are not inherently good. Both moves equip us with "high" and "low" side behaviors. The more conscious we become of these moves, the more we are able to consciously choose high side behaviors in stress and security.

Support center and reach center. Not only does the arrow moving away from our core type identify our stress move, but it also points to the Center of Intelligence that supports our dominant center, a.k.a. support center. In the first half of life (because life wisdom inevitably brings balance), we navigate the world primarily using our dominant and support centers. While Twos and Sevens are polar opposites in their positions on the Enneagram and their individual representation of feeling versus thinking, they share a doing support center which can lead to strikingly similar behaviors surrounding action and implementation.

In addition to identifying our secure move, the arrow moving toward our core type also hails from the Center of Intelligence that we need to consciously bring up or reach for in order to achieve balance among the three centers, a.k.a. our reach center. Five of the nine types have direct connection to all centers. For the four types whose lines give them access to only two of three centers (Fives and Sevens have no line to the Feeling Center, and Twos and Fours have no line to the Thinking Center), the secure behaviors of the numbers in their reach center provide a direct pathway to achieving balance.

Fives are able to seek balance in feeling once they engage productive doing in Eight and Sevens are able to seek balance in feeling once they slow down and engage grounded thinking in Five. Twos are able to seek balance in thinking after they connect with their own needs and feelings in Four and Fours are able to seek balance in thinking once they engage productive doing in One.

Our hardwiring exists independent of Enneagram discovery. This wisdom reveals what we already know about ourselves but may not have put into words or considered in the context of Centers of Intelligence. The lines that connect each of us to two other types are the key to achieving balance among the centers because they map the intuitive directions that we move to draw from other centers. This internal mapping is what informs our decisions and behaviors.

TRIADS AND PRIMARY TYPES

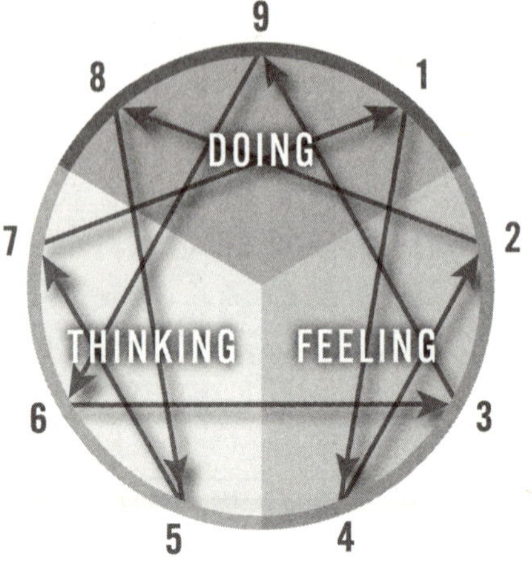

MUCH OF THE CONTEXT for the interpersonal understanding that the Enneagram provides lies in the groupings of three that permeate this motivational system. This space sets the tone for productive and meaningful collaboration in working environments. It is nearly impossible for an individual to be singled out when there are always two other types who share a similar outlook in any given situation.

Consider a confident, proactive executive who is being evaluated for a management position. The executive is paired with a more hesitant, cautious employee for a project that has a tight timeline. Company leadership has paired these two individuals in order to evaluate the swift processor's reaction to working with a slower processor. In the absence of Enneagram awareness, the executive is more prone to taking an autonomous approach that favors efficiency over collaboration—a move that will ultimately remove the executive from management consideration. Alternatively, if the executive has been equipped with the understanding that cautious hesitancy is a common characteristic of certain types and is not unique to the individual they have been paired with, the executive will be more prone to utilizing their own inherent strengths to facilitate effective collaboration.

Triads

Enneagram *triads* determine three factors that are central to our core motivation: the Center of Intelligence that we use first or most, the values that drive our daily decisions, and our fueling emotion. Each type's position on the Enneagram reveals the center used first or most, known as our filter or home base. Eights, Nines, and Ones employ doing first; Twos, Threes, and Fours employ feeling first; and Fives, Sixes, and Sevens employ thinking first.

Because we draw from all three Centers of Intelligence, values tied to centers that are not dominant can influence decisions, but the values in our dominant center emerge to drive decision-making. The fueling emotions of each triad are typical human emotions that can be experienced by every type. *Fueling* means that a specific emotion is free floating for the types in those triads and thus is the emotion we subconsciously employ as we move throughout our days. Subconsciously employing the fueling emotion leads the types in each triad to be the least aware of that emotion surfacing within themselves.

While Enneagram subsets reveal shared characteristics among types, traits that are unique to individual types, or non-negotiables, deserve focus as well. These non-negotiables are intrinsically tied to the motivating need for each type.

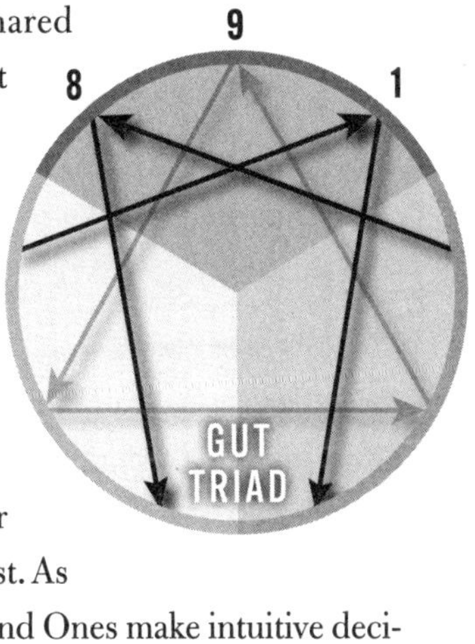

Gut Triad

Enneagram types Eight, Nine, and One are in the Gut Triad, where the Doing Center is the Center of Intelligence used first or most. As members of the Gut Triad, Eights, Nines, and Ones make intuitive decisions because they trust their gut. When types from other triads relate that they "trusted their gut," they more accurately trusted their heart (subjective view) or their head (objective reason).

The values that most influence decisions made by Eights, Nines, and Ones are tied to doing: effectiveness, functionality, implementation, and pragmatism. The fueling emotion for this triad is anger. All types experience anger, and the type to show anger and frustration with the most frequency after Eight is Six. So fueling has little to do with the rates at which they experience or display the emotion and more to do with the accessibility of that emotion and the sustainable energy it provides.

Enneagram Eights. While Eights, Nines, and Ones are the least conscious of anger when it surfaces, Eights have the most direct and honest expression of anger, facing the cause head-on the moment it surfaces. The non-negotiable for Eights, who are motivated to be against, is the reality that conflict energizes them. This does not mean that Eights seek out or cause conflict, and there are other types—Fives and Sixes—who are much more likely to engage in debate because they are contrarian by nature. When Eights engage in conflict, it usually surrounds injustice or lack of effort, and their anger is swift and transparent. Eights don't discriminate when it comes to the recipient of their anger and are usually unaware of the effects that the intensity of their delivery can have on others. Eights feel anger, express it in the moment, and move on, walking away from heated exchanges feeling energized and fortified. Because Eights do not generally see their intense reactions as a product of fueling anger, they are genuinely surprised when the world labels them as angry.

Enneagram Ones. One anger is internalized. They are motivated to be perfect, and the non-negotiable for Ones is pervasive inner criticism. Motivation to be perfect in an imperfect world leads Ones to settle for being good or right. Believing it imprudent to show anger outwardly (especially at work), Ones direct anger inward rather than acknowledging it when it arises. While we all have self-talk, the self-talk that Ones experience is consistently critical and fueled by righteous anger. Prompted by relentless inner criticism, Ones go through their days thinking of how they could have done better—how they could have responded to people and situations more productively.

When Ones internalize anger, it inevitably joins forces with inner criticism and morphs into resentment. Ones find themselves feeling resentful that others aren't doing their share or their part, aren't doing things the right way or following the rules. The stress line to Four in the Feeling Center means that feeling supports doing for Ones. Nowhere else on the Enneagram does feeling support doing, making Ones the most prone to taking criticism personally. As resentment grows, they intuitively look for fault in others in order to feel some reprieve. When Ones are criticizing you, be assured, whatever you are receiving has been applied first and worst to Ones themselves. When anger is finally released, it is usually in an explosive manner on those closest to them. It will not be what caused the anger initially, but it will be what tips the scales—traffic, the neighbor's noisy dog, the incorrectly folded towels.

Enneagram Nines. Many people are surprised to learn that Nines are in the anger triad because the world, in general, does not see Nines as angry. The non-negotiable for Nines, who are motivated to avoid, is their capacity to see both sides in a disagreement. Not only are Nines working to achieve internal peace, but they also are uniquely equipped to preserve harmony externally by mediating conflicting points of view. As a result, Nines are very laid back and easygoing, as we see them—although the Nine will tell you they do not always feel that way.

Many Enneagram authors have labeled Nines as passive-aggressive. I do not find anything regarding the motivation of Nines to be aggressive and prefer to use "passive angry" instead. The passive anger of Nines is generally expressed through silence and sweet stubbornness, a.k.a. the velvet wall. The reason everyone gets along so well with Nines is that Nines go along with the agendas of others. What others want to do sounds just as good to the Nine as what they might want, and they don't feel like they are giving up or sacrificing to merge with someone else's plan of action. That being said, Nines are not prone to peer pressure. Nines are much more decisive about what they don't want to do, and no amount of external pressure will change that.

My husband of twenty-three years is a Nine. Early in our marriage, if Billy and I were driving anywhere in the Dallas area and Billy was behind the wheel, it was likely that he was going slower than I wanted to go. If I asked him to move into a faster lane and he did not want to, what I received from him in those moments was warm regard. He would smile as if to acknowledge my request, turn up the volume on the radio, and stay right where he was in the right lane. He wasn't going to move, and we were not going to fight about it. Nines use sweet stubbornness to maintain harmony while signaling what they do not want to do.

In my early years of consulting, I would receive pushback when I singled out Eights, Nines, and Ones as the "angry" types in professional environments. Highlighting *anger* as the fueling emotion for this triad generally widens the gap between unapologetic Eights and others. It detracts from the focus of Ones who are uncomfortable with that particular exposure in front of their coworkers, and it confuses anyone working with Nines. This disconnect is bolstered by the reality that gut-centered types are the least conscious of their own anger.

Thus, in my training through the years, I have found *determination* to be a more accurate and relatable term for what fuels each of the members of the Gut Triad. Eights, Nines, and Ones all have a distinct way of digging in their heels. Determination for Eights and Ones surfaces in the ways that they want things done—to a certain standard and on a specific timeline. The determination of Nines surfaces when they don't want to do something—the velvet wall.

Primary Types

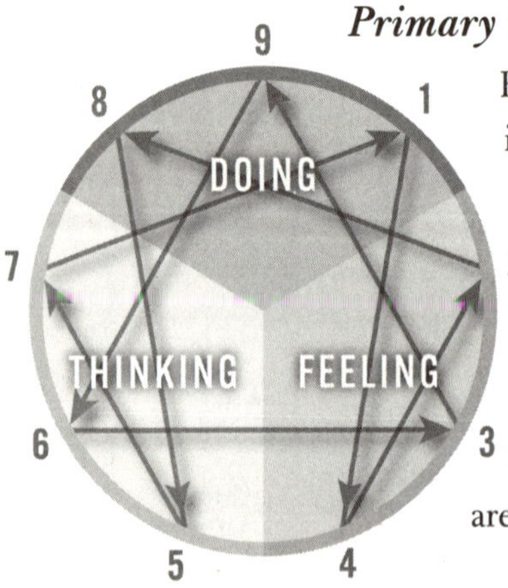

9
8
1
DOING
7
2
THINKING
FEELING
6
3
5
4

Before we view the remaining triads, it is important to identify the three types who use their dominant center *first,* but not *most.* These three types are the center point of each triad and are uniquely interconnected. When you look at an Enneagram, you see that, while all types are connected to two other types, these types are not all interconnected.

For example, Eights share a line with Five and a line with Two, but Five and Two are not connected. Ones share a line with Four and Seven, but Four and Seven have no connection. While this is true for six of the nine types, there are three types who *are* interconnected: Threes, Sixes, and Nines.

These types are called *primary types* and, while they utilize their dominant center to filter or take in what they are experiencing on a day-to-day basis, they do not inherently trust that center to process what they take in. Threes, Sixes, and Nines intuitively abandon their dominant center to process with a preferred center.

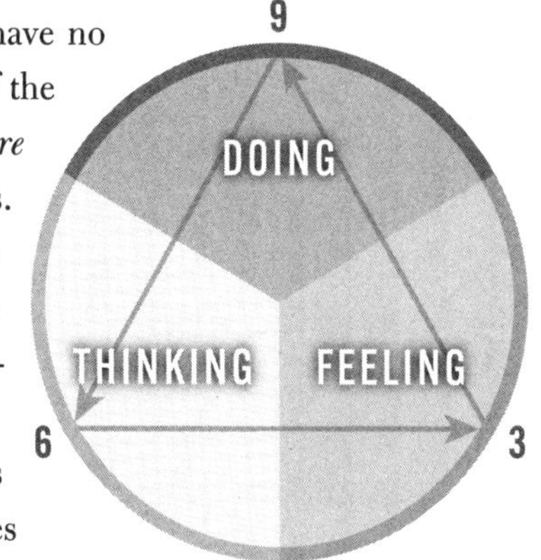

PRIMARY TYPES

Shifts for Primary Types. Primary types shift counterclockwise to process with a preferred center. Their dominant center serves as the home base, determining their fueling emotion and the values that drive their decisions. And while the shift to process with a preferred center follows their stress line, this shift is not a stress move. Stress and secure moves remain fully intact after the shift.

Nines take in the world through the Doing Center and void of stress, shift to process with thinking or objective reason. Nines intuitively trust their thinking more than their doing. Sixes take in the world through the Thinking Center and shift to process with feeling or their subjective read of the situation. Sixes do not trust the information or their thinking as much as they trust their ability to read their environment and the people in it. Threes take in the world through the Feeling Center before shifting to process with doing or action. Threes are not loyal to their emotions and do not have the confidence in feeling that they have in doing.

Acknowledging the stress line as a support center means that shifting to process with a preferred center disables the support center for the primary types. And primary types trust their processing center more than their dominant center, causing Nines to stay too long in thinking, Sixes to stay too long in feeling, and Threes to stay too long in doing.

As members of the Gut Triad, Eights, Nines, and Ones all approach the world with a doing filter and see when action needs to be taken. Because Eights and Ones process with doing, they roll up their sleeves and jump in, responding to what they see with action. Meanwhile, Nines trust their ability to reason objectively more than their doing. They sit back and think, *Someone should really do something about this.* It is not that Nines are oblivious to the situation. Preferred thinking means that Nines are better equipped to strategize a possible solution and are the type least likely to make themselves part of that solution. Nines spend an inordinate amount of time working things out in their minds before deciding to act while Threes shift into preferred doing, joining Eights and Ones to process with action. These doing processors are valued for their ability to make ideas functional.

Heart Triad

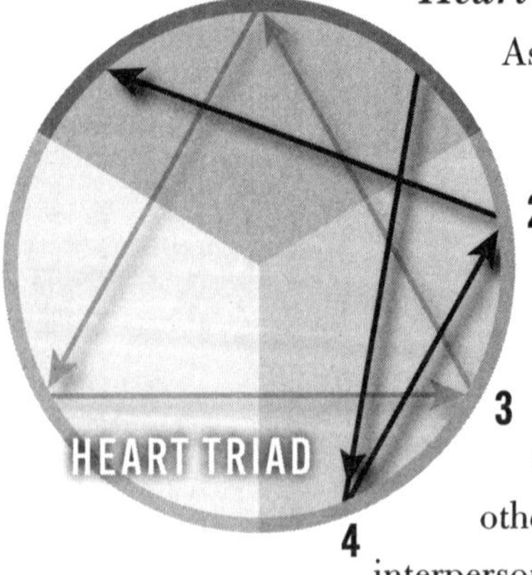

As members of the Heart Triad, Twos, Threes, and Fours use feeling first and Twos and Fours use feeling most. Because the Feeling Center is the people-centric Center of Intelligence, the values that drive the decisions of these feeling-dominant types are core to getting along with others: adaptability, emotional intelligence, interpersonal dynamics, and relationships. Twos, Threes, and Fours all possess a naturally high EQ. The fueling emotions for this triad are shame and anxiety, both of which stem from a general uneasiness within.

> As the primary type who shifts to process with the Feeling Center, Sixes mistype most frequently as Twos, Threes, and Fours. The first cue for a Six who has misidentified in this triad is to acknowledge their heightened awareness of personal anxiety. Heart Triad types tend to be the least conscious of anxiousness and rarely separate it from general uneasiness within.

Enneagram Twos. The non-negotiable for Twos who are motivated to be needed is the reality that they feel what others are feeling long before they connect to their own feelings. Twos are widely viewed as empaths because of this. Whether stranger or friend, if you cross paths with a Two and you are not okay, the Two will, in turn, not be okay. It is not until Twos learn the Enneagram that they begin to reconcile that most of what they feel on a daily basis are emotions picked up from others.

You rarely have to ask a Two for support. Because of their unique hardwiring, Twos sense what you need and set out to provide it, often before you realize you need it. While Twos are adept at sensing and meeting the needs of others, if you ask a Two what they are feeling, what they need, or how you can help them, those are three of the most difficult questions for a Two to answer. When Twos turn inward, uneasiness within keeps them from realizing for themselves what they so effortlessly offer to the rest of us. Like all members of this triad, Twos do not believe their value comes from within, so they measure self-worth through our appreciation for all the ways they give to us.

Enneagram Fours. While they are motivated to be understood, Fours are generally and accurately regarded as the most complex of all Enneagram types. Their complexity is grounded in natural uneasiness within and compounded by an internal focus. Unlike Twos and Threes, who avoid internal focus, Fours live most comfortably in their own world. The non-negotiable for Fours is that their emotions fluctuate at a much more rapid pace than other types. If we think about the moods and emotions that other types cycle through in the span of a month—a Four experiences the same cycle in a day or less. Fours often describe these fluctuations as feeling like they are on a swing or pendulum.

The internal focus of Fours ultimately leads them to see themselves in the light of their current mood. As their mood fluctuates, so does their view of themselves. All of this fluctuating is underscored by the very real feeling Fours have that they were born missing something integral to being content in the world. The other types have it, but the Four does not. As a result, Fours cannot help but see what's missing when their focus shifts to the external world. They are chronically disappointed, but rarely depressed. Complex.

Enneagram Threes. Threes are motivated to succeed and are hardwired to read the emotional tone of the room before adjusting themselves in response. The non-negotiable for Threes has two layers. First, Threes are able to disconnect from negative emotion, be it anger, shock, disappointment, sadness, or embarrassment. Second, Threes have a unique ability to project positivity to the outside world regardless of their own uneasiness within.

As the primary type in this triad, Threes take in but do not process with the Feeling Center. Filtering with feeling before processing with doing equips Threes with a natural ability to connect with others for the purpose of accomplishing goals and completing tasks. Because Threes miss out on a support center by doubling down on action, productivity is a must. Their uneasiness within is a major driving force behind their insistence on staying active. Stopping means stillness, and stillness means dealing with the growing piles of negative emotions that have been set aside.

Subconscious uneasiness within and filtering the world with a heightened awareness of others lead members of the Heart Triad to be fueled by comparison. Twos, Threes, and Fours are mentally comparing themselves to others as they go through their days.

Of the three types, Threes consistently, competitively compare. Twos and Fours can arrive at the competition that is born from comparison, but Threes start there. Threes are naturally the most competitive of all Enneagram types and their motivation to succeed is based wholly on comparison to others. The hardwiring of a Three asserts that one cannot be best unless they are better than.

Because Threes and Eights are both competitive doing processors who tend to look similar in professional settings, the illustration of running in a race is an effective way to delineate between the two. Threes are not equipped with an internal sense of best. Being fueled by competitive comparison means that Threes need to compete against other runners to be able to run their personal best. Not so for gut-centered Eights, who are largely unaware of others and are fueled by personal determination rather than comparison. An Eight will run with the same intensity whether they are running alone or against others. Once the race starts, Threes and Eights both want to win, and victory might involve running over others. The minute the Three crosses the finish line, medal around neck, they are circling back to whomever was in their path to help them up and make sure the relationship is still intact. Eights aren't equipped with the feeling or people-centric filter that Threes have, so the Eight has no reason to circle back. It's not that they don't care, Eights simply don't know that they ran over you.

The Feeling Center is utilized through subjective thought. For the types who process with feeling (Twos and Fours, and Sixes, the primary type who takes in with thinking before shifting to process with feeling), subjectivity governs mental reasoning. Regardless of the information provided, Twos, Fours, and Sixes make decisions based on how they feel, which is consistently tied to their awareness of who is involved. These types trust their feeling more than their ability to reason logically and are highly regarded for their ability to engage others.

Head Triad

The final triad is the Head Triad. As members of this triad, Fives, Sixes, and Sevens all employ thinking first, and Fives and Sevens employ thinking most. The thinking filter for these three types leads them to make decisions based on values tied to analysis, information, knowledge, and objective reason. The fueling emotion for the Head Triad is fear. Like anger, shame, and anxiety, fear is a normal human emotion experienced by all types. Because it is fueling for this triad, Fives, Sixes, and Sevens are the least conscious of their own fear. Fives fear a loss of autonomy, Sixes fear a loss of control, and Sevens fear a loss of freedom.

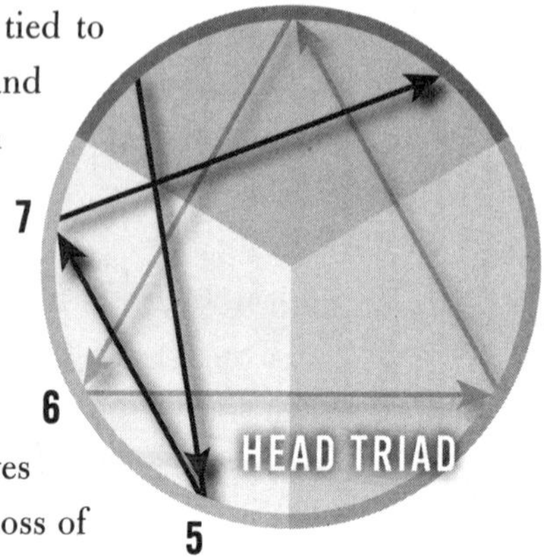

7

6

HEAD TRIAD

5

Enneagram Fives. The non-negotiable for Fives, who are motivated to perceive or understand a world where their point of view is often different from the crowd, is possessing an acute social battery. Energy measure is central to the Five's desire to control their own time and space. While Eights have the most energy of all types and Nines have the least, Fives have a finite store of energy. The singular element that reduces a Five's store of energy is human interaction. Being around other people, even if the Five chooses to be, drains that energy.

Fives and Nines look similar in professional environments. A key difference between the two is the energy that being around others provides. Nines often relate that they gain energy from being around others. Not so for Fives.

All interactions are costly in the private mind of a Five, so they spend their lives mentally weighing professional and social commitments against alone time. Fives give the rest of us cues when they are on empty. If their energy store is depleted while they are still obligated to be around others, the natural cynicism and sarcasm that all Fives carry internally flows outward. Fives in this space may use ill-timed humor and not recognize its effect on the room.

Enneagram Sevens. The non-negotiable for Sevens is their insistence on living life in the positive half-range of emotion. If you picture a range with the happiest and most euphoric feelings on one end and the saddest and darkest feelings on the other, Sevens who are motivated to avoid pain use thinking to stay on the positive end of the range. This mental move is called reframing, and it is the calling card of Sevens.

My husband, Billy, and I have two teenage sons, Will and Sam. Will is a self-identified Four and Sam is a self-identified Seven. One of my favorite Seven stories comes from Sam's years of playing soccer. At the age of eight, Sam was playing on a select team of boys who were all a year older. He had earned the starting goalie position and was a natural. (The effortless ability Sam has to excel, no matter the sport, has had the potential to be a sensitive subject through the comparative observation of our Four son as they have grown.) We were leaving a big tournament game one weekend, and while Sam's team had enjoyed a semi-final win bolstered by his performance in goal, his Eight mother (who will go all out to support others as long as they give their very best) thought he could have stopped one of the goals that got by him. When Sam was settled in the car after the game, our conversation went like this: "Sam! What a game. That was an awesome win, and you did so well! What happened with that first goal?" Without pause, Sam replied, "Mom, I don't remember goals that are scored on me."

The tendency that Sevens have to reframe negatives into positives leaves them naturally upbeat and optimistic. It must have been a Seven who coined the phrase FOMO (fear of missing out). Sevens delight in the most positive and numerous possibilities—there is no such thing as too much.

I had a Five teach me years ago that while Sevens have FOMO, Fives have JOMO: joy of missing out. This Five shared that she loves when plans get canceled because she gets unexpected time back to be alone and take care of her limited energy store.

Enneagram Sixes. As the primary type in the Head Triad, Sixes value information and analysis and are prone, like all Head Triad types, to look for patterns in life. Though hardwired to be the least conscious of their own fear, Sixes recognize inherent doubt and the ability to always see another angle as the catalysts for their perpetual preparedness. The non-negotiables for Sixes, who are motivated to feel secure, are offering superfluous context and having a contingency plan. Because they value information, Sixes are always asking questions, but Sixes trust their preferred feeling, or subjective view, far more than thinking or data. They appreciate a free flow of information and need time to decide how they feel about that information before making a big decision.

It is important to note that Sixes struggle most to identify their Enneagram type because they see themselves in all types and are the only type to draw from a span of behaviors to reconcile a singular motivation. The behaviors Sixes employ to meet their intuitive need to feel secure can stand in stark contrast to one another. While a focus on authority is consistent, the Six response to authority takes one of two paths. Sixes who regularly adhere to authority and place their full trust in the system are referred to as *phobic*. Sixes who consistently doubt authority and are willing to rebel against the system are referred to as *counterphobic*. Counterphobic Sixes widely misidentify and are mistyped as Eights.

Sixes who lean more counterphobic tend to mobilize beyond their doubt much faster than those who lean more phobic. In reality, all Sixes have the innate ability to draw from phobic and counterphobic behaviors as they navigate the world. Most Sixes can identify times in their life when they ran toward perceived danger in order to overcome anxiety and feel secure (counterphobic) and when they ran away from perceived danger in order to feel secure (phobic).

The expression of fear in the Head Triad is as different for Fives, Sixes, and Sevens as the expression of anger is for Eights, Nines, and Ones in the Gut Triad. Thus, a better term for what fuels Fives, Sixes, and Sevens is *anticipation*. Fives anticipate what the outside world is going to require from them and mentally compartmentalize their energy reserves in response. Sevens derive their energy (and they have a lot) from delightful anticipation. While not all Sixes anticipate worst case scenarios, all Sixes anticipate what could go wrong.

With Sixes shifting away from the Thinking Center to process with preferred feeling, Nines join Fives and Sevens to process with objective reason. Thinking processors are valued for their levelheadedness and ability to see the big picture.

While these subsets tend to share few commonalities with respect to observable behavior, a basic grasp of triads and primary types is foundational to successful application of this system and makes all the difference for anyone looking to motivate others in a work or social environment.

PROCESSING CENTERS AND STANCES

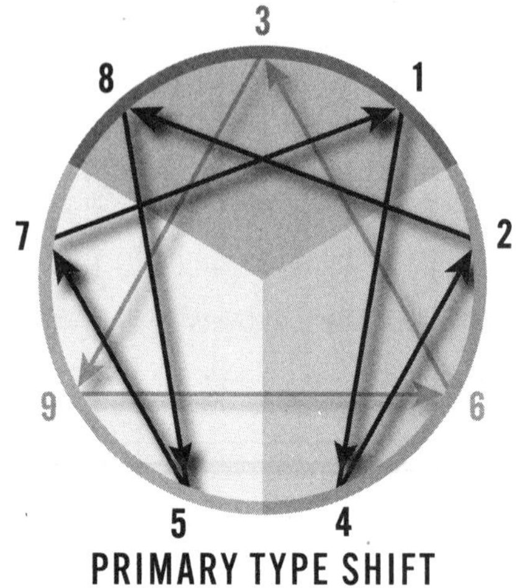

PRIMARY TYPE SHIFT

ENNEAGRAM TYPES IN BRIEF	
1s	Motivated to be perfect. Lives with consistent internal criticism.
2s	Motivated to be needed. Feels others' emotions before recognizing own.
3s	Motivated to succeed. Disconnects from negative while projecting positive.
4s	Motivated to be understood. Fueled by rapidly fluctuating emotions.
5s	Motivated to perceive. Operates with a limited social battery.
6s	Motivated to feel secure. Offers superfluous context and ready with a contingency plan.
7s	Motivated to avoid pain. Lives life in the positive half-range of emotion.
8s	Motivated to be against. Energized by conflict.
9s	Motivated to avoid. Able to see both sides in disagreement.

WHETHER YOU ARE JUST LEARNING the types or you need a review, here's a quick summary of each type with a focus on the core motivation for each.

After understanding triads and primary types, learning the concepts of *processing centers* and *stances* is essential to typing self and others with accuracy. While triads explain what is not observable, processing centers and stances speak to much of what can be seen in others. Processing centers and stances thus present terrific ways to analyze whether individuals have been positioned to influence their environments positively based on inherent gifts.

The shift of primary types (Three, Six, and Nine) to process with a preferred center presents an alternate visual for consideration: processing centers.

Doing Processors

While we are all "doing" at work, Eights, Ones, and Threes are processing with action and implementation. Doing processors are considered "motors" because they are valued in the workforce for their ability to make things happen. If a company is struggling to meet a strategic goal of sustainable growth, stagnancy can often be attributed to a lack of motors. Eights, Ones, and Threes should be represented in the decision-making body for growth to be an actionable priority.

> I consulted the executive staff of a holding company for years prior to working with the employees of the subsidiaries. During those years, the growth of one of the subsidiaries lagged considerably in comparison to the others. Once I gained access to the leadership team of the company that had fallen behind, I found no Eights or Threes and three employees who had mistyped as Ones.

Feeling Processors

Feeling processors are extremely valuable because they are the most in-tune with client feedback and employee needs. Twos, Fours, and Sixes have the most accurate read on the pulse of an organization when it comes to the well-being of clientele and personnel. Involving these feeling processors in decisions that affect culture and client engagement is paramount.

Thinking Processors

It can be overwhelming to consider how many decisions are made by the most emotionally or physically invested types in an organization

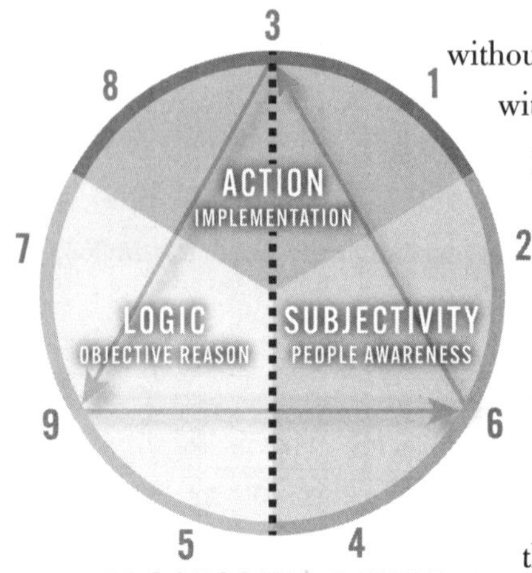

without much input from those who process with logic and objective reason. When you consider the thinking processors, the tendency of Sevens to keep things light and on the surface can prevent them from being considered or regarded for their intellectual depth. Fives and Nines are internally referenced. Unless time and space are provided for Fives and Nines to offer their objective input, they are prone to keep it to themselves.

Processing Divide

When considering the Enneagram from a processing centers perspective, there is a natural divide among employees on the right—who bring a combination of doing and feeling to work, making decisions with a subjective mindset—and employees on the left—who bring a combination of doing and thinking to work, making decisions with an objective mindset. Based on their tendency to double down on preferred doing, Threes straddle the divide. Threes can slow down to engage with others on the right side of the divide and they can slow down to engage the Thinking Center on the left side of the divide, but both moves for balance require slowing down, which Threes are the least prone to do. As a result, Threes may find themselves somewhat removed from the inevitable disconnects that occur between individuals on either side of the processing divide.

Stances

Stance understanding is extremely insightful when it comes to bringing the three intelligence centers into balance. Just as triads determine three factors central to core motivation, so do stances. Stances determine the Center of Intelligence we use least or last, our orientation to time, and our reference point. Since we all have the ability to look at our lives in the context of the past, present, and future, orientation to time is better understood as our mind's default. Our reference point tethers us internally, externally, or independently and has a lot of influence on decision-making.

Each of the three stances has a type from each of the three triads. While we can present very differently from our triad counterparts, we share noticeable similarities with our stance counterparts. We tend to have the most in common with the types in our stance because we generally approach the world in similar ways. While individual Enneagram type can be identified once the age of an individual reaches double digits, stance presents much more clearly in early childhood, as early as the ages of two to four.

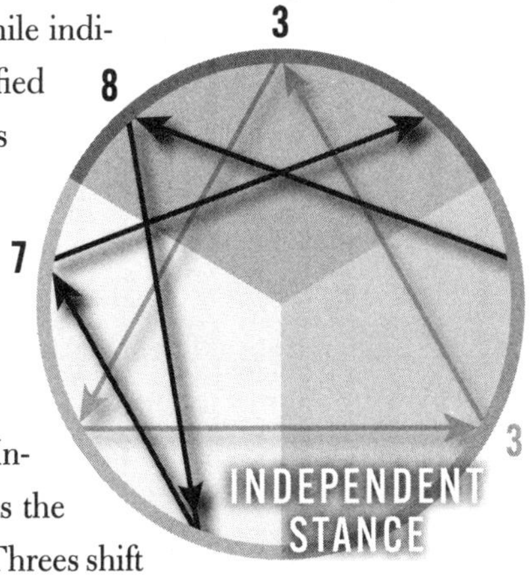

Independent Stance

Threes, Sevens, and Eights share the Independent Stance, often referred to as the Aggressive or Assertive Stance. Once Threes shift to process with preferred doing, not only are these three types aligned as a stance, but their position on the Enneagram also reflects the greatest distance from the Feeling Center, providing a terrific visual for the center that these types use least or last. Since Enneagram type is based on motivation, it is important to note that, while the members of this stance are no more aggressively behaved than other types, Threes, Sevens, and Eights are all aggressively motivated to get their way and assume that others will follow their agendas. Subjectivity and people awareness—elements that can be drawn from the Feeling Center of Intelligence—are rarely considered when forming those agendas. Threes, Sevens, and Eights live most easily in the illusion of control. This is because they don't tend to get distracted by the input of other people when making decisions, and they are not influenced by emotions—their own or the emotions of others.

Eights process with doing supported by thinking (line to Five), Sevens process with thinking supported by doing (line to One), and Threes abandon feeling to double down on doing. All three types are fast processors and big-picture thinkers who are drawn toward action and excitement. They have the highest self-confidence, the most energy for action, and the highest stress thresholds. Independent Stance types think fast, move fast, and have the least patience for the slower pace of other types.

Orientation to time for Threes, Sevens, and Eights is the future. For Eights, this typically manifests in large-scale problem solving. For Threes, it is setting and surpassing personal and professional goals, and for Sevens, it is the fueling anticipation of limitless options and new experiences.

The reference point for the members of this stance is neither internal nor external. For Threes, Sevens, and Eights, who share the same general response to the distractions that captivate or repel the attention of others, their reference point is independent. The world could be blowing up (metaphorically, of course) next to a Three, Seven, or Eight. They can choose to respond to the explosion, but they can also stand right next to the explosion and remain unaffected by it. They are able to stand independent from it.

Members of this stance benefit most from consistency in a professional environment. Because their independent nature drives elevated self-esteem, providing consistency for Threes, Sevens, and Eights in the workplace prevents the illusion of control from prompting these confident, independent types to take over.

Responsive Stance

The opposite of the Independent Stance is the Dependent or Responsive Stance. This stance consistently represents half of the corporate population because it likely represents half of the general population. If the world is blowing up next to a One, Two, or Six, they cannot stand independent from it. These types are motivated to respond to what is happening outside of them because, while they did not choose it and cannot change it, Ones, Twos, and Sixes all have an external reference point. They intuitively feel responsible for improving what they see.

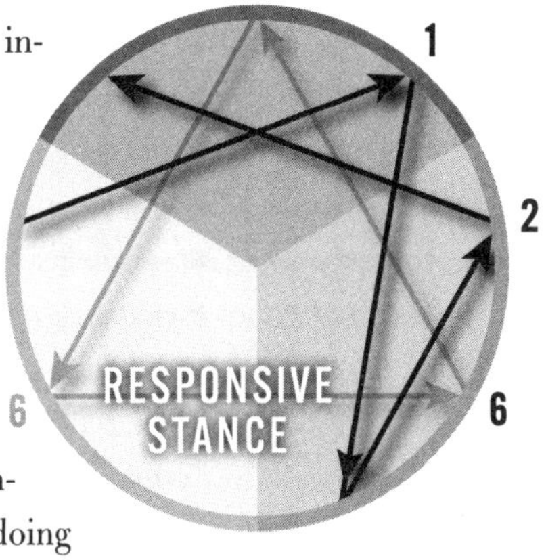

Once Sixes shift to process with preferred feeling, these three types are aligned on the Enneagram and are farthest from the Thinking Center, which is used least or last. This imbalance is not a reflection of intellectual capacity, but the reality that doing and feeling are working in tandem and separate from thinking. Ones support doing with feeling (line to Four), Twos support feeling with doing (line to Eight), and Sixes abandon thinking to double down on feeling. Thinking least or last means that Ones, Twos, and Sixes struggle to objectively evaluate their efforts and rely on setting high standards like attention to detail to assure the quality of their work.

One of the clearest benefits gained from utilizing the Thinking Center is personal boundaries. Consider Fives in the Thinking Triad, who are often regarded as the most logical and objective type. Fives unquestionably have the strongest personal boundaries—they have no problem saying no. Utilizing the Thinking Center least or last means that Ones, Twos, and Sixes generally have the worst personal boundaries. These types find it difficult to say no and often take on more than what is theirs to do because they feel strongly about responding to what is outside of them. While all types in this stance struggle with boundaries, Twos struggle the most because they have no direct connection to the Thinking Center—no line to Five, Six, or Seven.

The orientation to time for this stance is the present. Ones, Twos, and Sixes can all be ruled by the demands of the immediate. Being oriented to the present and having a natural deference to their external environment lead the members of this stance to think out loud or verbally process as they respond to what they encounter on a daily basis. As a result, these types prefer time and space to talk through their thinking and bounce ideas off coworkers. It is important for the rest of us to broaden our awareness and patience when we work with members of this stance. Cutting off or interrupting a One, Two, or Six is cutting off more than words—it often interrupts the chain of thought, leading them to start over or repeat themselves.

Members of this stance benefit most from affirmation in a professional environment. Affirmation can be interpreted in a myriad of ways, so a good rule of thumb is to practice active listening with Ones, Twos, and Sixes. They often reveal the affirmation they are seeking through their verbal processing.

Solitary Stance

While the reference point is independent for Threes, Sevens, and Eights and external for Ones, Twos, and Sixes, the internal reference point shared by Fours, Fives, and Nines places them in the Withdrawing or Solitary Stance. Once Nines shift away from doing to process with preferred thinking, these three types are aligned and are farthest from the Doing Center, the center they use least or last. While Fours, Fives, and Nines tend to have the least physical energy, as a group, drawing from the Doing Center least or last does not mean that the members of this stance aren't doing. These three types can be very active and accomplished. Doing least or last means that they generally do what they like and what they want, in the order that they like and want, and on a timeline of their choosing. Any outside pressure to the doing of Fours, Fives, and Nines—which comes with every job and much of life—results in an intuitive stubborn response. These types intuitively push against being told what to do, how to do, or when to do.

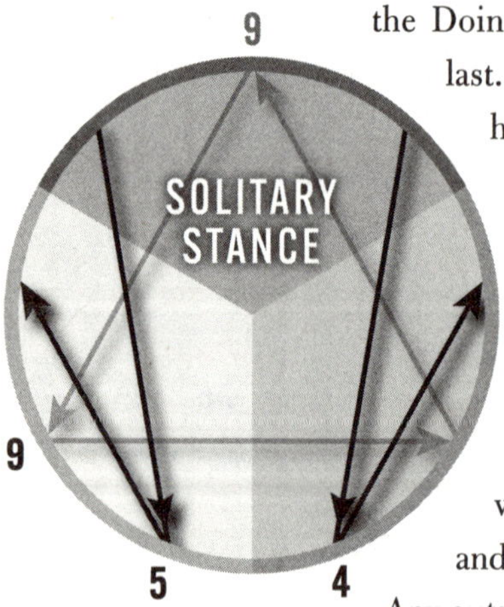

Their internal reference point means that Fours, Fives, and Nines find comfort by pulling inside of themselves and away from the world. They can withdraw at any given moment during a meeting, a conversation, or a gathering. As a result of this intuitive ability to withdraw, Fours, Fives, and Nines all think that they engage and speak with the rest of us more than they actually do. They'll give extensive thought to what they might say, but the words may not leave their mouths. Their ability to withdraw internally is often mirrored externally. If they don't live alone, these three types usually have a place in their homes where they retreat to be alone.

Orientation to time for Fours, Fives, and Nines is the past. Much of their mental energy is tied to past experience. Future planning that involves a plan of action can be very taxing for these types. With doing being engaged least or last, consistent routines end up being very helpful for these types and ultimately allow for more productive doing (see the discussion of "baseline doing" in the chapter on Nines).

Members of the Solitary Stance have less in common when compared to the shared traits among members of the other two stances. Once these types withdraw from outside stimuli, there is a strong internal distinction between Fours, Fives, and Nines.

When Threes, Sevens, and Eights stand independent from outside stimuli, they continue to share common traits. Ones, Twos, and Sixes are all responsive to outside stimuli and are similar in the ways they share responsibility for what they see. The recognizable commonalities of Fours, Fives, and Nines are limited due to the reality that an internal reference point makes them difficult to read.

Members of this stance benefit most from latitude in a professional environment. Because these types are internally referenced, others tend to be more intrusive with them when searching for a desired response. Disregarding personal boundaries will inevitably end in a stalemate when working with Fours, Fives, and Nines.

If you embrace the idea that all types are necessary for any collective group to function at its best and acknowledge that every type deserves a seat on "the bus," processing center consideration ensures everyone is in the right seat, and stance consideration keeps everyone on the bus engaged, satisfied, and moving in the same direction.

PART I SUMMARY AND QUICK REFERENCE

	Triad	Filter	Fueled by	Processing Center	Stance	Center used least or last	Orientation to time	Reference point	Work best in environments that offer
1s	Gut	DOING	Determination	DOING	Responsive	THINKING	Present	External	Affirmation
2s	Heart	FEELING	Comparison	FEELING	Responsive	THINKING	Present	External	Affirmation
3s	Heart	FEELING	Comparison	DOING	Independent	FEELING	Future	Independent	Consistency
4s	Heart	FEELING	Comparison	FEELING	Solitary	DOING	Past	Internal	Latitude
5s	Head	THINKING	Anticipation	THINKING	Solitary	DOING	Past	Internal	Latitude
6s	Head	THINKING	Anticipation	FEELING	Responsive	THINKING	Present	External	Affirmation
7s	Head	THINKING	Anticipation	THINKING	Independent	FEELING	Future	Independent	Consistency
8s	Gut	DOING	Determination	DOING	Independent	FEELING	Future	Independent	Consistency
9s	Gut	DOING	Determination	THINKING	Solitary	DOING	Past	Internal	Latitude

THE ENNEAGRAM AT WORK

Shifting from a macro perspective in part one to a micro perspective in part two, we will turn our focus to each of the individual types in the workplace. Adhering to the foundational wisdom of Enneagram triads, individual types will be presented in the following triad order:

Gut Triad

- Eight—The Challenger
- One—The Perfectionist
- *Nine—The Mediator

Heart Triad

- Two—The Helper
- Four—The Romantic
- *Three—The Achiever

Head Triad

- Five—The Observer
- Seven—The Enthusiast
- *Six—The Loyalist

*primary type

ENNEAGRAM EIGHT

I didn't come to work to make friends.

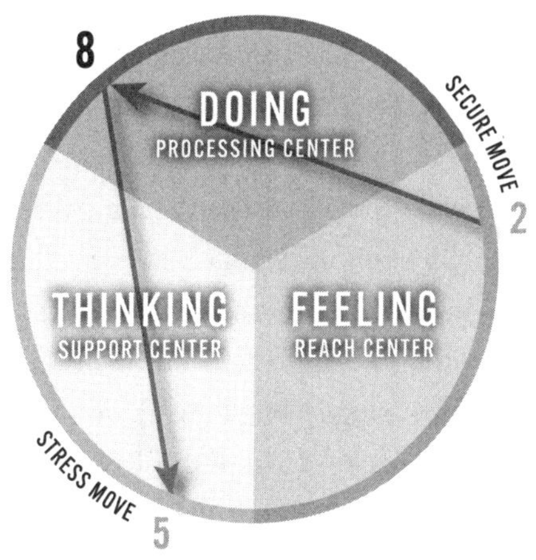

8s HOW EIGHTS VIEW THEMSELVES AT WORK	HOW OTHERS CAN VIEW EIGHTS AT WORK
I am self-confident.	You are arrogant.
I make things happen.	You are reckless.
I am decisive.	You are dismissive.
I have high standards.	You are hard to please.
I am passionate.	You are overbearing.
I am direct, blunt, and firm.	You personally attack others.
I don't have time for chit-chat.	You think only of yourself.

THERE WAS A DISTINCT PATTERN to my professional reviews for the first twenty years of my career. Regardless of the industry or my specific role in the organization, the message was the same: "Joey, we cannot do what we do at such a high level without you . . . and you have to get along better with others." In other words, my doing was unparalleled, my thinking was innovative, but my feeling had to improve. Applying the Enneagram to this reality helps. Through the lens of the Enneagram, I understand that I intuitively bring the Doing and Thinking Centers to work and leave the Feeling Center at home.

I envision employers utilizing a metaphoric scale in their ongoing assessment of Eights. We thrive on productive doing and we have endless energy and ideas for making things bigger and better. Making sustainable growth an exciting reality is part of the hardwiring of Eights. These intuitive gifts heavily tip the scales in our favor. As our time in any organization passes, the hurts and slights that we unwittingly cause others begin to accumulate on the other side of the scale. Coworkers who bring feeling to work outnumber Eights as much as ten to one in most cases. Most of those who bring feeling to work have an external reference point. Without being consciously aware of it, these types do not let up in their scrutiny of the unaware Eight until a tangible restitution has been achieved.

Due to high autonomy and comfort in conflict, it would not occur to an Eight to approach Human Resources about a coworker. Ironically, most grievances about Eights that are brought to Human Resources departments (HR) by others are a result of the Eight offering to others what we want in return: directly addressing our issue with the specific person without involving anyone else.

Self-Confidence Versus Arrogance

When I was in my early twenties, I was in a room where my mother was teaching the Enneagram and, as she was talking about the self-confidence of Eights, someone in the room made the unsolicited offer that Eights have "egregious" self-confidence. To this day, I remember my anger in that moment—anger that covered a more vulnerable but familiar feeling of being completely misunderstood. How could my *self*-confidence be flagrantly bad or offensive to others?

In truth, members of the Independent Stance (Three, Seven, Eight) have the highest self-confidence, but Threes have ingrained relatability by filtering with the Feeling Center and Sevens approach others with social awareness and versatility. Eights don't lead or follow with relatability—we have to consciously reach for it, making us generally the most misunderstood type. And Eights have a well-cultivated sense of being right. While that sounds egregiously self-confident, it is statistically accurate.

Eights are the only type for whom action is supported by objective reason (stress line to Five), making us problem solvers by nature. Add that we are extremely fast processors who don't get bogged down by emotions, and the results are logical and actionable solutions offered quickly and without feeling. When Eights offer a solution, we know it will work and, perhaps as important to note, we don't need buy-in or affirmation from others. But Eights don't walk away from solving a problem patting ourselves on the back. We don't offer solutions to be regarded as more important or better than. Arrogance implies superiority and superiority requires comparison, which is simply not part of the Eight mindset. Comparison is rooted in a focus on others that Eights do not employ.

Regardless of these truths, Eights are the most intimidating type, making it incumbent upon Eights to extend ourselves to engage with others. Eights are placed in leadership positions early and often. Generally, what catapults us to these positions is connected to doing and thinking. Therefore, it doesn't occur to us to draw from feeling while we are leading. When we authentically utilize our Feeling Center to connect with coworkers, our natural stance of intimidation eases. When Eights make a conscious effort to join the groups we inevitably lead, the results can be powerful.

Making Things Happen Versus Being Reckless

I work with a company led by a male Eight. Their motto is "living on the edge of chaos"—language that makes the Six in Human Resources (who thrives on predictability) very uncomfortable. This Six has shared that she feels like she represents the brakes in the organization because her Eight leader "never lets off the gas." This company is successful by the Eight's standards—their bottom line grows exponentially year after year. On the other hand, the Six measures success through culture health and community buy-in, making her view of success unattainable when employee turnover is consistently above 30 percent.

Eights are generally impatient with the rest of the world while we move at warp speed. We expect others to jump in and keep up or get out of the way. The Eight need to be against, fueled by determination, leads us to aggressively meet challenges head-on. This energy tends to feel personally combative to others. When someone tells an Eight that a certain task cannot be done on a short timeline, the Eight squares up against the timeline, ready to infuse our natural gifts into defying the odds and making it happen. Inevitably, the person who doubted—usually an advisor or manager of the Eight, takes this move personally and feels like the Eight squared up against them. But we were defying the odds and thus are truly confused when you accuse us of defying you.

Fives and Eights are the only two types who do not intuitively draw from feeling or responsiveness at work.

I always reflect fondly on a seven-year period in my professional history when I reported to a Five. Not only was he the ever-neutral constant when I dipped into low side Two behavior and was emotionally reactive, he was never overwhelmed with my fast processing and appreciated my big picture vision. His patient, logical approach to doing served as a natural guide, often without me realizing it. I can only imagine the ways that he advocated for me behind closed doors, responding with objective reason to those who came to him with any number of subjective slights they may have felt as a result of my haste to make things happen.

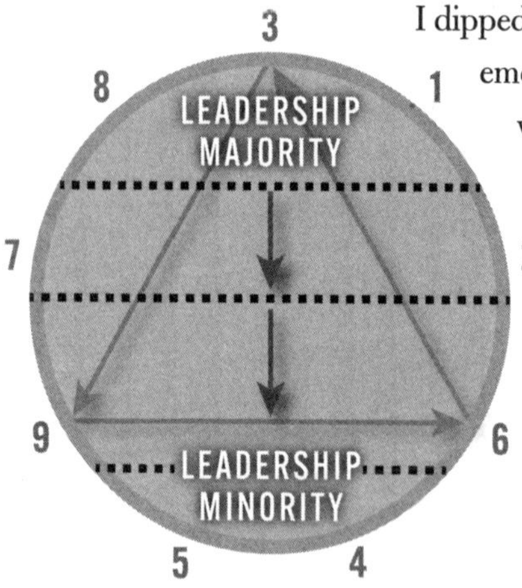

3
8
1
LEADERSHIP MAJORITY
7
2
9
6
LEADERSHIP MINORITY
5
4

PRIMARY TYPES SHIFT
TO PROCESS WITH THEIR PREFERRED CENTER

3s PROCESS WITH ACTION
6s PROCESS WITH A SUBJECTIVE VIEW
9s PROCESS WITH OBJECTIVE REASON

Sadly, the world rarely provides Eights with a Five advisor. The more I consult in corporate America, the more I find leadership positions largely fill from the top of the Enneagram down.

If you are an Eight, there is a lot to be gained on both sides from consistently engaging with a Five in your organization whom you trust and respect.

Being Decisive Versus Being Dismissive

Eights are easily the most decisive type. Being gut-centered underscores that decisiveness because we trust ourselves. When anyone who is struggling to figure out their Enneagram type offers that they "might be an Eight," their indecisiveness is typically a sure sign that they are not. Simply put, we Eights know ourselves and we don't waiver when we make decisions.

Being unhesitating can create discord in the workplace without the Eight realizing it. Unrealized impact is a common theme when discussing Eights at work. We do not realize how we affect others because we are not affected by others. This is the biggest hurdle separating Eights from achieving balance among the Centers of Intelligence.

> As members of the Feeling (or human-centric) Triad, Twos, Threes, and Fours are all naturally equipped to read and get along with others. Sixes and Sevens lead with social awareness and Ones lean into responsiveness, making them acutely aware of how they come across to others. As Withdrawing or Solitary types, Fives tend to fly under the radar, escaping the scrutiny of coworkers, and Nines get along with everyone as an unspoken rule.

When you tell an Eight in a professional environment that we hurt your feelings, our line to Five leads us to self-reflect objectively. The decisive response that invariably follows sounds something like this: "I know, without a doubt, that I didn't mean to hurt your feelings. Therefore logically, if your feelings are hurt, that's on you." If you can believe it, that's actually a more mature Eight response. I admittedly cringe when I am in rooms with young misunderstood Eights who, when put on the spot to answer for a coworker's hurt feelings, react decisively with varying versions of "suck it up," "stop being a baby," or "I don't care."

In those moments, it is clear that the young Eight has grown weary of being part of a game they didn't know they were playing—where everybody else seems to know the rules but did not inform the Eight. Eights are often blindsided by the emotional reactions of others. In the Eight work mindset, feelings are not a priority. If we are required to deal with your feelings and you believe we hurt you intentionally, you don't know us. You didn't make an effort to get to know us. You likely shared your feelings with any number of uninvolved but interested parties before you told us (or had someone else do it). Therefore, you don't deserve what little softness and vulnerability we have to offer.

Enneagram understanding reveals that none of us can change how we see the world. Consciously bringing three centers into balance does not alter who we are and can go a long way in improving how we interact with others. Eights of all maturity levels need to make an effort to draw from feeling at work because it does not diminish our doing or thinking but rather elevates it. One of the simplest ways to extend ourselves to others is to slow down and listen first. Patience is a virtue. While the concept of developing virtues in the workplace may not be prioritized in the for-profit sector, it tends to be a non-negotiable in nonprofit environments, an employment category that has grown 33 percent in the last fifteen years, surpassing local government to become the second-largest source of employment in the country. Regardless of the expectations that accompany an Eight's work environment, developing patience can lead others to value our decisiveness by removing the distraction of feeling dismissed.

The concept of leading with patience and listening to others before offering a solution is easier said than done. As forward-thinking, lightning-fast processors, Eights have usually resolved the issue before others arrive at the realization that there is an issue to be addressed. Providing space to process out loud benefits every type in one way or another.

Ones, Twos, and Sixes need to verbally process to connect with thinking; Fours, Fives, and Nines benefit from verbally processing a plan of action. Even fast-moving Threes and Sevens benefit from talking things through. Sevens are much more likely to engage fully if a brainstorm session precedes action, and Threes who tend to double down on doing will not utilize thinking without being encouraged to slow down and strategize first.

Having High Standards Versus Being Hard to Please

Eights might be the only type to view micromanaging as being too relational. When I reflect on my own managerial style over the years, I am aware that those who reported to me would probably have liked a bit more direction to follow my consistently lofty expectations. If you report to someone who places emphasis on the minutiae of how you get tasks accomplished, you are not dealing with an Eight.

Eights do everything at a very high level and assume others are striving to as well. We have extremely high expectations of ourselves and our environment and wouldn't dream of lowering those under any circumstance. A typical motto for Eights who are attempting to relate to the rest of the world is, "Do better." Meeting the unspoken expectations of an Eight with any sort of consistency can be daunting if you are not motivated to see like an Eight and don't have the energy or drive that Eights have.

The two elements that fail to meet an Eight's expectations with the most regularity are attention to detail and scope of impact. When you consider the doing processors, while Eights share the most similarities with Threes, attention to detail is one of the few areas where Eights and Ones align. For Eights, this is a key benefit to being the only type for whom doing is supported by thinking. Eights fit attention to detail into our natural swift execution, whereas Ones can get bogged down by it, slowing productivity and leading them to micromanage. Threes tend to bypass attention to detail, cutting corners in their drive to be efficient. This consistently proves to be the number one stressor for Ones who work with or manage Threes. Over time, Ones can become extremely resentful of cavalier Threes who receive applause for completing tasks by cutting corners while speeding through doing. Not so with Eights. We do plenty to irritate Ones, but sacrificing detail for speed is not on that list.

Scope of impact ultimately means that Eights have big ideas and the confidence to execute these ideas successfully in a big way on even the shortest of timelines. At one time in my career, I took on a golf tournament that raised money for tuition assistance at a local private high school. The tournament had run successfully for years, so anyone could step in and repeat what had been done and get similar results. As the product of a Title IX upbringing (see the introduction to the chapter on Twos), I wanted an exponential increase in female and alumni participation. With less than six weeks to prepare, I added tennis and bunco tournaments. Two weeks out, I had the idea to thank golfing sponsors with a custom-logoed cooler filled with drinks preferred by each member of the sponsor's foursome that were not available on the course.

At no point did I consider tabling these ideas for future tournaments nor did I adjust my expectations to fit what could "reasonably" be done in a short time. It was suggested that we add tennis or bunco, but not both. Several offered that we could add the coolers without logos and fill them with the course drinks on hand. With terrific joint effort, my team pulled off the largest and most successful tournament to date. The addition of tennis and bunco increased female and alumni participation by 400 percent. Participants talked about the logoed coolers with preferred drinks for weeks after, ultimately increasing sponsorship for the next year.

There is no task too menial for an Eight. We don't ask anything of others that we are not jumping in to do ourselves. Often, other types who work with or for Eights get overwhelmed by our big ideas and unwavering drive. Instead of acknowledging that Eights are hard to keep up with, these types may default to believing that Eights are hard to please.

Being Passionate Versus Being Overbearing

Eights have the most energy on the Enneagram. We give 150 percent to everything we do, and we are all in or all out. This reality contributes to our natural intimidation of others. It can be difficult to relate to someone who moves and thinks as quickly as an Eight and only takes notice of you when you meet us with similar energy.

Eights are loud. We speak at a high volume and default to superlatives. We are a larger-than-life presence even when we are consciously governing our intensity. "All in or all out" means we are big in the room or we are not in the room at all. I have a distinct memory of a coworker telling me in my early twenties, "You just want to yell and be loud." If an Eight ever wonders how we are regarded by others, it doesn't get much simpler than that.

I used to genuinely struggle when my mom would teach that Eights "love to pick a fight." That never hit home for me. I resonate a great deal with conflict being energizing, but starting conflict for the sake of conflict never settled well. Then I had an epiphany that changed the way I viewed that message and my interactions with others. It occurred to me that when I walk away from a heated exchange with someone, I regard the exchange as a good talk. Eights don't advocate for anything that we are not passionate about. Why should we see things from your side if you are not equally as passionate? If voices are raised, all the better! What I considered a fruitful or productive conversation was considered a fight by everyone else's standards.

I consult an Eight who was reported to HR (story of our lives) for using all caps in an email. The reporting party felt that they were "being yelled at." The Eight was dumbfounded. How else was he supposed to write FYI?

Someone once told me, "To know an Eight is to love an Eight." There is beautiful truth in those words. Eights let very few people get close enough to know us, leaving most of the world to make up their mind based on what we allow them to see. While we cannot change our innate desire to keep our circle small, Eights can slow down and consider how our intensity is going to be received by others. The energy boost we gain from that heated interaction on the front end will never be worth the amends the world requires us to make for our perceived tyrannical approach on the back end.

Being Direct Versus Personally Attacking Others

One clearly definable constant for Eights in professional environments is the accusation of personal attack. This accusation never ceases to amaze me. The Eight says to others, "You are not doing your best work," or "You can and must do better." And others reply, "You can't talk to me like that," or "You personally attacked me." At no point were words that were mean spirited or specific to any part of that person uttered.

There is an unending list of reasons why I love being married to a Nine. The reason that tops that list is his ability to explain me to others in a relatable way. Billy has said, for years, that if you take the court reporter's transcription of what I say, it is honest, to the point, and void of personal insult. He continually reminds me, as he reminds others, that I lose others in my delivery.

Because unrealized intimidation is a common thread for Eights, the unforgiving term that finds its way into our personnel files most often is "bully." This can be extremely difficult for Eights to reconcile. In our purview, we are much more likely to take on the bully than be one. We are fierce advocates for the underdog and readily step in to defend those who might struggle to defend themselves. Even the most surface analysis of the psychological makeup of a bully reveals low self-esteem—not possible with Eights.

Nevertheless, we have to be aware of how we come across to others. I consulted an Eight years ago who experienced issues with her delivery as Head of Nursing. Staff reviews accused her of being emotionally inconsistent. Upon thorough examination, she discovered that her staff did not like being "jumped" for not meeting her expectations and then invited to join her at the cafeteria table in the same shift. What her staff didn't understand was how she could feel so strongly about their performance in one moment and not carry that feeling beyond its expression.

People are confused when they hear that Eights are not angry. We express our anger as intensely as we feel it and then we move on. We don't stay angry once the issue is addressed. What we miss altogether is the staying power of our delivery. As the chief advancement officer of a private high school, I was admonished in a formal review for "not being pastoral with employees who had a poor perceived work ethic." While it is safe to assume that the Catholic deacon who wrote that review was speaking through the subjective veil of spirituality, his words were a stinging reminder twenty years into my professional career that I still had much to learn. Regardless of titles or the religious (or nonreligious) affiliation of employers, this will always be an Eight's work to do. Two of the best decisions an Eight rising in management can make are to censor our reactions and create buffers. When Eights are motivated to directly address an employee who does not report to them, they should refrain and approach that employee's manager or find another way to address the situation instead of the individual.

Eights need buffers. We don't have the relational bandwidth to build connections with a large number of people who will trust and respect us enough to not take our delivery personally, but we can do it with a few. Those important few serve as valuable intermediaries between us and the organizations that we are trying to build to thrive independent of us.

Not Having Time for Chit-chat Versus Thinking Only of Ourselves

Early in my career, I had a direct report tell me that working for me was like working in a factory. Since Eights are the only Enneagram type to carry a double task focus to work (see the chapter on Threes), that makes sense. Eights typically experience tremendous success in forward- or client-facing positions. If external relatability is required to do our job at a high level, Eights are able to intuitively draw from feeling and connect with others with ease. Engaging someone else as a function of what an Eight has been tasked to do is as natural as it is energizing. On the other hand, telling us that we need to extend ourselves to connect with others who are peripheral to what we are trying to accomplish feels awkwardly burdensome and taxing.

I consult a company that hired an Eight to be a recruiter in HR. She was masterful at engaging high-level recruits to fill open positions but was regarded as aloof in the limited time that she was actually on campus. She consistently excelled beyond her peers in her recruiting efforts, often receiving unsolicited praise from new employees who lauded her authentic and enthusiastic engagement as one of the principal determinants that led them to choose employment with that company. When asked for my input, I answered with a standard Eight question. Is she doing the job that you hired her to do? The resounding yes for her literal job description ended up being overshadowed by the no for her implied job description—buying into employee culture in a way that was clearly observable by all. She is no longer employed with that company.

From a logical perspective, Eights are the only type on the Enneagram who have no self-focus. I have spent a lifetime reminding others, often after discovering that my behavior has been discussed at length by others, that not focusing on them in no way meant that I was focusing on myself. I now have language for that. My focus naturally shifts from task to task before shifting to others.

If the Enneagram has taught me anything, it is that the world does not operate from a logical perspective, especially when it comes to getting along with others. Extending myself to connect with a colleague requires intentionality on my part. I want Eights to learn, as I have, that needing to adjust our minds to engage our hearts doesn't diminish the authenticity of our engagement with others. And the return on investment is greater than we can imagine.

TIPS FOR MANAGING OTHERS, AS AN EIGHT

The intent of your message gets lost in the delivery of your message.

- While you are quick to react, be intentional about being slower to speak.
- When you feel motivated to address an issue the moment you become aware of it, step back and think about your approach and delivery.
- Before addressing a coworker, ask yourself, How will my words and delivery make this person feel?

Offering to others the consistency that you desire does not account for the needs of others.

- While Threes and Sevens appreciate your consistency, they rarely share your expectations for output. Attention to detail should be taught and not expected.
- Ones, Twos, and Sixes make up half of the population—this means you are working with a large number of people who need affirmation and like feedback. You don't require either, so you must make a conscious effort to offer it to others.
- Fours, Fives, and Nines do not share your penchant for swift reaction when it comes to doing. Extending latitude means working to establish mutually agreed upon timelines for work completion.

What got you to leadership won't keep you there.

- You rise quickly in organizations bolstered by action and sound judgment. Being an effective manager requires social awareness and versatility.
- Lean into others' perspectives with curiosity. You are the fastest processor and a natural problem solver, and your distance from feeling can limit your awareness of the personal toll that your swift and direct approach can take on others.
- You cannot effectively lead a group that you do not join. Make a habit of getting to know the members of your team.

TIPS FOR MANAGING AN EIGHT

There is no such thing as too direct.

- When you sugarcoat or beat around the bush, you lose. Avoid mixed messages.
- If you have an issue, address it as soon as possible and with minimal outside input.
- Be clear and concise with your expectations.

Your aim is mutual respect.

- Stop needing Eights to like you. That is relational currency that Eights don't bring to work.
- An Eight who does not respect you will stand independent from you. Being the authority means being consistent, it does not mean being louder or more intense.
- Avoid superfluous praise. Eights don't need your affirmation.

Learn to recognize the difference between intensity and anger.

- Eights are intense. A reactive Eight is passionate about solving the problem. When others take their passion personally, it confuses the Eight.
- The intensity of an Eight does not obligate you to address the issue on their timeline. Eights rarely recognize their way of being in the world as intimidating. When you set the response time, it gives you both a chance to assess the situation without emotion.
- Find your own voice when you go toe to toe with an Eight and employ objective reason as much as possible.

ENNEAGRAM ONE

My work is an extension of who I am.

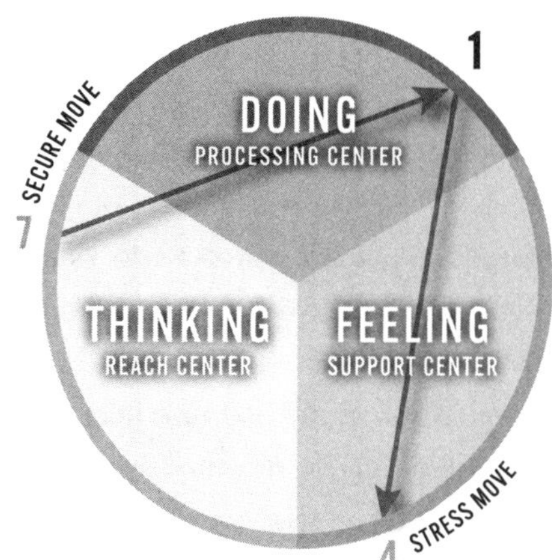

1s HOW ONES VIEW THEMSELVES AT WORK	HOW OTHERS CAN VIEW ONES AT WORK
I am improvement minded.	You are critical.
I am detail oriented.	You micromanage.
I value accountability.	You have unrealistic expectations.
I work for the good of all.	You overstep.
I appreciate checks and balances.	You are untrusting.
I hold myself and others to high standards.	You are judgmental.
I am conscious to avoid mistakes.	You cannot take criticism.

I HAVE OFTEN REFLECTED that, while Enneagram understanding has nurtured my compassion for all types, I have the most compassion for Ones. I truly cannot imagine the burden of being motivated to realize perfection in such an imperfect world. Add the reality that Ones are the only type for whom feeling supports doing, and we can begin to comprehend how and why Ones feel so strongly about their actions and the actions of others. If perfection is the end goal and anger is the fueling emotion, righteous frustration is inevitable.

While Eights share a triad and processing center with Ones, their penchant for action and standards for doing are not impeded by others. In other words, Eights are not distracted by others as they focus on the task. Ones are acutely aware of others, yet that cognizance will never supersede a motivation to do what is right in a way that is right. Alternatively, consider Twos, who share a Responsive Stance with Ones and represent feeling supported by doing, and whose processing center is so intrinsically tied to others, that cultivating or preserving a relationship can override their standards for action.

Enneagram wisdom recognizes the inner turmoil of Ones as a consistent struggle with their critic. I find that internal struggle for Ones to be significantly compounded by an external reference point. Not only are Ones destined to wrestle with relentless self-judgment, they also carry the exhaustive weight of seeing how much better the world outside of them could be. Learning the Enneagram and discovering that the rest of us do not share this improvement lens can bring clarity to the struggle but certainly doesn't alleviate it.

Being Improvement Minded Versus Being Critical

Imagine waking up every day feeling personally responsible for improving everything you encounter. From the minute you step out of the fog of sleep until you manage to quiet your mind enough to sleep again, your days are filled with an anxious desire to refine, tweak, and correct what you see. You rarely consciously consider this to be a burden—it is simply how you see. Your responsive nature makes you comfortable, if not enjoyable, to be around. You are considerate and kind and you easily make connections with others. What others do not see is your unrelenting internal critic, tapping you on the shoulder at every turn to remind you that you will always top the list of what could be better.

It is extremely difficult for Ones to extricate themselves from their critic. In truth, Ones believe that the critical voice they carry with them is largely responsible for the good that they do in the world. Quite often, Ones who are raised in any number of Christian traditions come out of childhood mistakenly believing that critic to be the voice of God or the Holy Spirit. To have criticism so deeply ingrained in a motivation to be perfect ultimately means that Ones are unable to hold one without the other. They wonder how any of us can improve without such guidance. Ones realize that their own critic is unkind, and so the guidance that they offer to the rest of us ends up being deliberately distinct from what they experience internally.

The subjective thinking of Ones often surfaces in the mental energy they devote to delivering criticism in a way that can be received well by others. I work with a licensed professional engineer who makes a point to edit drawings with blue ink, though the industry standard (and his preferred color) is red. Like most Ones I consult who manage others (and most Ones do), he is perpetually aware of how he is coming across and considers his delivery with such care that when his suggestions are not well received, he bears the weight as much, if not more than, the recipient. When we accuse Ones of being critical, we tend to do so without considering that our barometer for receiving criticism is starkly different from their own.

One of the best ways we can extend understanding to the Ones we work with is to consider that, while the criticism they offer us is temporarily tied to the task or project, their self-criticism is ongoing. Whether we take their feedback to heart or dismiss it, labeling it as critical signals to Ones that they have missed the mark.

Being Detail Oriented Versus Being a Micromanager

We all possess the ability to be controlling in any given situation. As members of the Independent Stance, Eights, Threes, and Sevens control with self-confidence, high energy, and swift processing. Solitary types (Nines, Fours, and Fives) control through stubbornness and a shielded internal reference point. The external reference point of Ones, Twos, and Sixes in the Responsive Stance makes them the most outwardly (and thus recognizably) controlling. Of the three Responsive types, Ones uniquely process with doing.

Ones filter and process with the center that is the most difficult to counterfeit. Human beings can convincingly feign concern for others (feeling) or rational thought (thinking). It's arguably more difficult to feign measurable productivity. The reality of Ones' inability to stand independent from the way tasks are accomplished contributes to their desire to control the process. When we observe higher functioning or more balanced Ones in a business environment, the upside of this desire is that they make excellent trainers. On the downside, this desire in a lower functioning or less balanced One reveals itself in one of two ways: micromanaging or refusal to delegate.

Ones are meticulous in every sense of the word. Their devoted attention to detail—bolstered by dualistic thinking and perfectionist tendencies—leads them to see the "right" way to do something. This is precisely the space where a natural lack of objectivity becomes the Achilles' heel for Ones. When the perfectionist feels so strongly that their way is the best or only correct way to accomplish a task and is unwilling to consider an alternate course of action, reason has been left behind. Leading with this subjective view and an inability to ignore what is in front of them causes Ones to over involve themselves in minutiae on their quest for rightness.

Enneagram understanding teaches us that we cannot change how we see, only what we do with how we see. That being said, constructive application of this understanding must include setting each other up for success. Ones are usually content to lead by example among their peers. Promoting Ones to manage others exponentially increases their personal scope of responsibility. If effective leadership includes taking ownership for the mistakes of the team, no other type is more naturally equipped to do this than Ones. But at what cost?

I consulted a team of hospital physicians and administrators over a period of three years. In that time, a nurse on staff who identified as an Enneagram One was promoted to Nursing Director. Following her promotion, a chief administrator asked me to meet with the One amid growing complaints from her direct reports, the same nurses who had applauded her rise in the ranks. I discovered that her promotion did not include an office change. This One was now directing a team of nurses from the same close proximity that she had worked with them as peers. Her own stress over the situation was poignantly palpable when we met.

I encouraged the chief administrator to move the One, noting that it would be impossible for her to reach her management potential if she continued to work in such close proximity to her direct reports. I encouraged the One to assign tasks and then walk away rather than giving in to her desire to observe those in her charge complete the tasks. The key here is recognizing the need for an adjustment on both sides. Utilizing Enneagram wisdom requires more than identifying imbalance and adjusting behavior. None of this works if we fail to recognize and honor the nuance of unvarying motivation.

Valuing Accountability Versus Having Unrealistic Expectations

It is likely that we have all worked with a One and regarded their expectations as unrealistic in one way or another. So often, what others consider to be unrealistic comes from the One's verbal processing and desire for consensus. Part of being in the Responsive Stance means that Ones, Twos, and Sixes value feedback, especially at work. These types function well in systems where they can consistently gauge being on the right track through discussion. As the doing processor in the Responsive Stance, Ones utilize discussion to maintain consensus in their actions and the actions of others. Other types aren't wired to believe that accountability requires agreement, and many of those types find verbal processing to be laborious.

Because Ones are emotionally connected to being right about the best course of action, their pursuit of consensus can be exhaustive. The agreement that Ones seek must come from the concessions of others because Ones feel too strongly to concede themselves. Accountability starts with verbal agreement to do something the way the One wants it done and continues with check-ins from the One until the task is complete. This specific brand of accountability—transparency combined with a desire for consensus through discussion—tends to interfere with the autonomy that others desire as they move through their own task lists at work. Such interference leads others to view Ones' version of accountability as flawed or unrealistic.

Ones and Eights share the view that accountability requires transparency, a notable distinction from the Nines who complete the Gut Triad. To explain this distinction, one must consider Enneagram types from a joint triad and stance perspective. As members of the Independent Stance, Eights represent independent action, which ultimately means that their doing is transparent and cannot be influenced. Extending this reasoning to the Responsive Stance reveals that Ones represent responsive doing. Ones' actions are also transparent but can be influenced thanks to their external reference point. That leaves others to regard the solitary actions of Nines, who represent doing that is neither transparent nor influenceable.

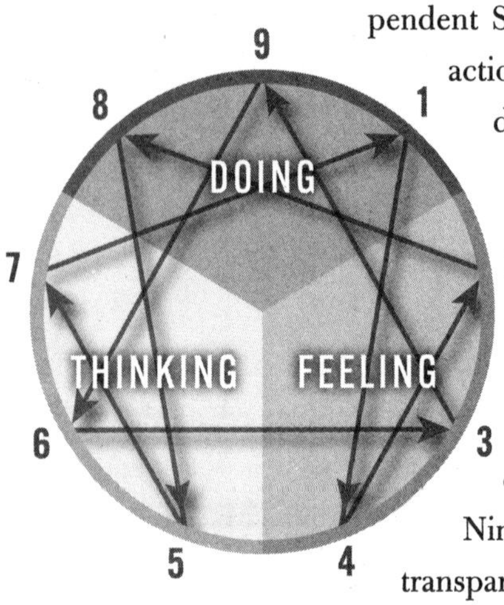

The shared lines on the Enneagram ultimately determine whether our thinking, feeling, and doing is independent, responsive, or solitary. If Eights represent independent doing, so do Twos and Fives. If Ones represent responsive doing, so do Fours and Sevens. If Nines represent solitary doing, so do Threes and Sixes. Taking into account the reality that there are more Sixes and Nines than any other type means that a significant portion of the world does not view accountability as a function of transparency.

Regardless of influenceability, transparent doing for Eights and Ones guides them to be naturally straightforward with a plan of action. The added external reference point of Ones equips them with a radar, of sorts, for doing. This is precisely where the Ethic of Reciprocity can lead to disappointment. Ones operate by sharing a discernable path forward and expect others to do the same, especially at work.

Working for the Good of All Versus Overstepping

If the common thread for the Responsive Stance is subjective action that is grounded in an awareness of others, it should come as no surprise that Ones see themselves as doers for the collective good. One of the most consistent personal struggles I find with Ones in any work environment is feeling isolated or disconnected from others when their uncompromising standards for doing create natural separation. This struggle is undoubtedly what sets Ones apart from the other action processors. The human-centric Center of Intelligence that supports doing for Ones is utilized least or last by Eights and Threes, who are both able to stand independent from others while doing.

Working for the good of all generally reveals itself in one of two ways for Ones: first, taking on more than what is theirs to do and second, struggling to delegate tasks to others. The licensed professional engineer whom I mentioned earlier tells a story about when one of his direct reports informed him that he would not be able to finish a project by the agreed upon deadline. This One responded by doing what most, if not all, Ones would do in his position. He worked overtime to complete the project himself.

It makes sense that we can encumber the Ones with whom we work when we do not share their scrutiny for task completion. We unwittingly burden them much more when we do not consider our own actions as necessary for the collective good. In other words, Ones are used to seeing what and how something should be done with a clarity that others do not typically share. What Ones have difficulty reconciling is any motivation for doing that is not intrinsically tied to working for the good of all. This is usually the space where resentment rears its head. Ones internalize anger to avoid laying it on others. Ironically, much of what Ones do to avoid disconnection with others eventually causes the disconnect.

When Ones take on more than what is theirs to do or choose not to delegate, both strategies reveal a desire to connect with others by working for the collective good. They seek connection by wearing themselves out to improve what they see while making a conscious effort not to burden the rest of us. It is understandable then that Ones might struggle when others' response is to deny connection by accusing them of overstepping and doing too much.

Appreciating Checks and Balances Versus Being Untrusting

When I am working with a company that is newer or going through a transition that would benefit from streamlined processes, I look for input from Ones first, followed by Sixes and then Twos. An often-overlooked advantage of utilizing logic least or last is being uniquely equipped to implement systems and processes. After all, who needs to slow down and utilize objective reason when you have proven systems in place?

Remember that Ones value efficiency and effectiveness while meticulously avoiding mistakes. As dedicated rule followers, they rely on procedures that regulate workflow. The competency mindset of Ones leads them to elevate the process over the individual. Starting with themselves, Ones are keenly aware of the ways that humans can be prone to error. This awareness is often received by others as a lack of trust. On the other hand, systems and processes, when implemented correctly, are much less susceptible to missing the mark.

The unforeseen issue that often arises when Ones elevate process is that they may not accurately account for individual liability. Responsive types (Ones, Twos, and Sixes) have to be cognizant not to "throw the baby out with the bathwater" when human error interferes with established protocols. I consult a holding company run by an Enneagram One. Shortly after I began working with this One and his leadership team, there was an expense account issue with an employee in one of the subsidiary companies. Rather than target the issue within the singular company, he directed finance to implement policy changes that affected the expense account process for all subsidiaries. This move had a ripple effect where employee trust was concerned. The leadership in each affected company had to deal with their own interpretations of the move as a lack of trust from the One before dealing with similar reactions from their employees.

The swift reaction time of Ones to remediate system breakdowns is a valuable attribute in any working environment. Improved productivity is quantifiable and follows the rise of most Ones in business. An inevitable byproduct of such a blanket approach is that those who work with and for Ones can be left feeling like they have to repeatedly prove themselves following someone else's blunder or misjudgment. What the One sees as efficient error-proofing is often received by others as misplaced mistrust.

Having High Standards Versus Being Judgmental

You would be hard-pressed to find anyone with higher standards for work output than Eights and Ones. This directly correlates to Eights and Ones being the only two types who take in and process with doing.

> If you carry this reasoning to the Feeling and Thinking Centers, Twos and Fours arguably hold the highest standards for authentic emotion and treatment of others, and Fives and Sevens hold the highest standards for logic and objective reason.

While Eights and Ones share elevated standards for doing, their intuitive response when those standards are not met differs based on their positions on the Enneagram. Eights lean into dismissiveness while Ones lean into judgment.

> A common thread exists between dismissiveness and types on the left of the processing divide (Fives, Sevens, and Eights) and judgment and the types on the right of the processing divide (Ones, Twos, and Fours). Since primary types (Three, Six, and Nine) are interconnected and actively shifting through the Centers of Intelligence, they are more susceptible to a milder form of both reactions.

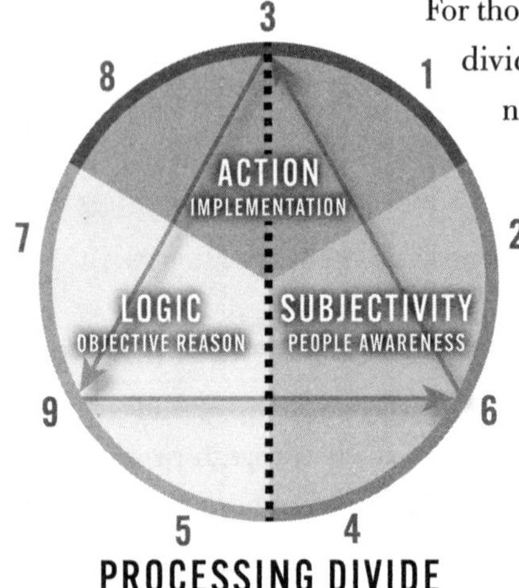

For those types on the left of the processing divide, valuing autonomy over connection to others can lead to being dismissive of others when expectations are not met. For those on the right of the divide, valuing connection over independence can lead to being judgmental of others when expectations are not met.

Another non-negotiable trait indicative of Ones is black-and-white or dichotomous thinking. This type of thinking for any individual categorically leads to unrealistic expectations and emotional distress. Because feeling uniquely supports doing for Ones, emotional distress directly correlates to having high standards. When Ones are so certain that their plan of action is the only way or the best way forward and are unwilling to compromise, that inflexibility is a clear indicator that objective reason is not being employed. It is highly subjective to believe that your way of doing something is the only viable option. Bringing thinking into balance with doing and feeling ushers Ones into the gray areas that they are hardwired to reject. Flexibility is a universal signal that Ones are consciously drawing from thinking.

Being Conscious to Avoid Mistakes Versus Being Unable to Receive Criticism

I was promoted to manage a small team for the first time when I was in my twenties. Having only been on the receiving end of professional reviews up to that point in my career and knowing that, as an Enneagram Eight, my bluntness could be intimidating, I took great care to consider my approach for each team member.

I started the review of the event coordinator on my team with confidence. I had prepared a glowing review that accurately reflected her work. She was efficient and organized and shared my passion for doing at a high level. I commended her for all the ways she elevated our team. I thanked her for being someone I could consistently count on to do her job and do it well. While we had not discussed the Enneagram, her work ethic, engaging energy, and thoughtfully crafted appearance led me to believe that she was likely a Three. I celebrated her attention to detail when it came to organizing events and did not consider until much later the meticulous care that she took to create spirals of perfectly formatted to-do lists with perfectly symmetrical check boxes next to each item.

We enthusiastically collaborated on our aligned visions for how to execute events at a level that surpassed what had already been publicly acknowledged as the best in our industry. Then I began to discuss her one area for growth. Her passion led her to, at times, be aggressive in her approach with employees who had been tasked with supporting our events but did not share our vision for excellence. I offered a brief history of professional reviews that arrived at similar suggestions for my own development. After all, we had bonded over undeniable parallels in our approach to work up to this point, why not share an area for growth? The more I talked, the less she did. As her demeanor shifted, red splotches began to appear on her chest and rise up her neck to her face. I had prepared a professional review with a Three in mind, but she was a One.

When working with Ones, it is imperative to remember that what they offer to the rest of us in terms of criticism barely scratches the surface of the relentless internal flogging that Ones endure day to day. More often than not, our criticism of Ones is met with passionate defense. It is an intuitive move on their part to delay the beating they are perpetually poised to give themselves. When constructive criticism is the aim, rather than speaking first, ask the One for their summary of the exchange or task or event and then listen without interrupting. Ones do not do anything without shrewd analysis before, during, and after their contribution has been made. When you give them the space to verbally process their thoughts, nine times out of ten, Ones will offer your criticism for you, and you can take it from there.

TIPS FOR MANAGING OTHERS, AS A ONE

Nobody feels as strongly as you do about the task at hand.

- You are the only type for whom feeling supports doing. Wanting others to care as much as you will only lead to disappointment and judgment.
- Practice accepting approaches that are not your own. When you are so sure that your way is the best or only way, you are not employing objective reason.
- Acknowledge your anger in the moment. Whether you write it down or say it under your breath, naming the source of your anger, when it arises, will ease building resentment and explosive episodes.

It is impossible to improve everything. Don't set yourself up to feel like you failed.

- You cannot change your external reference point, so you will always be aware of what is happening outside of you. Sometimes you need to adjust where you choose to look.
- Consistently figure out what "good enough" means to you and then stick to it.
- When you begin to feel overwhelmed, hopeless, or both, do not ramp up doing to escape those feelings. Practice stopping or slowing down instead. The feelings will subside (and so will the critic).

Others can learn a lot from you. Be aware of the ways you facilitate disconnection.

- Threes, Sevens, and Eights do not need agreement to move forward and will not be convinced by long-winded arguments. Be clear with your non-negotiables and then move on.
- While Twos and Sixes share your elevated standards for doing on the front end, they do not share your penchant for going back over something that has already been done. Be

careful not to drag them along when you choose to audit after the task has been completed.

- Fours, Fives, and Nines do not like to be told what, when, or how to do something. Communicate your expectations early and concisely, and avoid multiple check-ins.

TIPS FOR MANAGING A ONE

There is no such thing as too specific.

- Ones are meticulous doers and will struggle if the job requirements are vague or lack purpose. Set and maintain clearly defined expectations.
- Ones appreciate efficiency and order. Offer step-by-step instructions when introducing a new task.
- Ones believe in earned achievement. When Ones ask you what they can do to be considered for promotions, be specific.

Affirmation goes a long way with Ones, and it does not mean a pat on the back.

- Give Ones the space to ask questions and verbally process their thoughts.
- Maintain an open-door policy that accommodates Ones' need for continuous feedback.
- Ones want to know they are contributing to the greater good. Rather than highlighting their efforts, find ways to honor the impact of their efforts.

You will never scrutinize Ones more than they do themselves.

- Ones spend their days thinking of how they could have responded to people and tasks more productively. They notice error that the rest of us do not see. When you offer feedback, do not shy away from jumping into details with them.

- Ones are honest with themselves and others and want you to be honest with them. When they ask you for input, be straightforward and detailed with your response.
- When you want to offer criticism, first ask the One how they thought it went, and steer the conversation from there.

ENNEAGRAM NINE

Can't we all just get along?

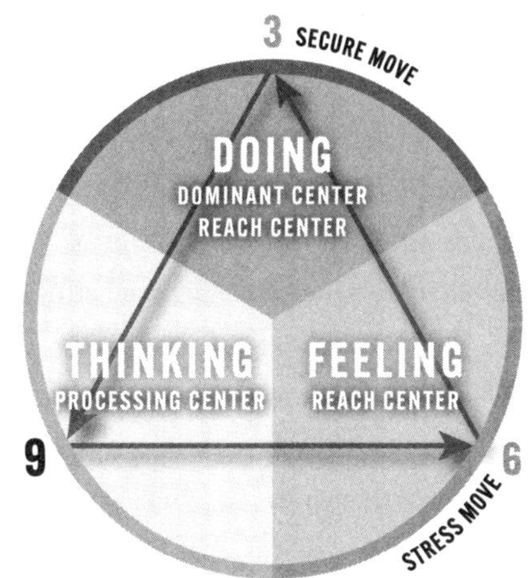

9s HOW NINES VIEW THEMSELVES AT WORK	HOW OTHERS CAN VIEW NINES AT WORK
I am methodical.	You are slow.
I have positive presumption for others.	You are unable to have hard conversations.
I take time to process before speaking.	You are unresponsive.
I get along with others.	You are a pushover.
I don't like to voice disagreement.	You are passive-aggressive.
I find it satisfying to complete simple tasks.	You procrastinate.
I see multiple sides to any situation.	You are indecisive.

MY HUSBAND AND I both pursued careers in education. Individual circumstances led me to private parochial education and led Billy to public education and charter schools. At one point in our lives, the high school where I was employed began searching for a new principal. I was sure that Billy would be a terrific candidate. Knowing that my Enneagram Nine husband does not respond favorably to being told what to do, I was deliberate with my approach, dropping subtle hints to him to consider applying. One of my fellow administrators at the time knew Billy well and also gently nudged from his side. There was no movement from Billy.

Just as I was escalating my efforts to encourage him, Billy sat me down and lovingly explained to me that he would never work in the same building as me for the sake of our relationship—something that he valued more than any job would ever be worth. He reminded me that he represented the type of person that I struggled most with in work environments.

And he was right.

One of the most common management struggles that I encounter in consulting involves dealing with Nines and our very real misconceptions of them at work. Nines do a terrific job of getting along with others. They are not disrespectful or insubordinate, they harmonize conflicting points of view, and they are inherently good-to-the-core human beings. It is difficult for most of us to reconcile being consistently frustrated with someone who is often the nicest person we've ever met. How do you address an employee who needs to improve when you can't quite put your finger on a specific and actionable grievance?

Being Methodical Versus Being Slow

I used to think I was giving Nines their due when I would anchor my description of them with "Slow and steady wins the race." I then had a Nine in Wisconsin offer the mantra attributed generally to the military and specifically to Navy SEALs: "Slow is smooth, smooth is fast." As a swift-processing, high energy Eight who fits easily into the breakneck pace of American culture, it might not surprise you that I still prefer to use "slow and steady" when I teach this type. Being the daughter, sister, and wife of Nines further precludes me from ever using *fast* when referring to them in any context.

The correlation between a slower pace and moral high ground has been made for centuries. Buddhism, Daoism, and Confucianism all celebrate the virtues of a slow and deliberate life. Entering "slow living" or "The Slow Movement" into any search engine produces an abundance of literature from all corners of the globe recognizing the innumerable benefits of reduction in every aspect of life, starting with speed. When you consider the elevated position of Nine on the Enneagram symbol, it makes sense from a spiritual or philosophical point of view. Nines are hardwired to embody a path to enlightenment that is historically and globally revered yet has little to no place in the broadly accepted definition of a successful business model.

The determination that fuels Nines is the most obvious in the space where culture demands speed and the Nine simply resists. Eights, Nines, and Ones are all fueled by determination. As two of three types who process with doing (Threes being the third type), Eights and Ones tend to dig in their heels most in the ways that demand action from themselves and others. Being the primary type in the Gut Triad means that Nines are fueled by determination, but do not process with doing, shifting to process with a preferred Thinking Center instead. Nines are resolute in the ways that they control their own time and space and will not be moved to act in a manner or at a pace that is not of their choosing. In other words, determination fuels doing for Eights and Ones and fuels not doing for Nines.

My husband has equipped me with some terrific terminology in my quest to understand and teach Nines. He often refers to the importance of what he calls "baseline doing." Though they might push against it internally, all Solitary types (Nines, Fours, and Fives) can experience tangible benefits from establishing and maintaining a consistent routine. Method, process, and routine all fit into the category of baseline doing, and Billy insists that, without it, productive doing for Nines is impossible. Drawing from the Nine wheelhouse of objective reason, this idea makes a lot of practical sense, so why does it tend to be rejected as inefficient in the workspaces that Nines occupy? The answer likely lies in our cultural preoccupation with speed and excess whereas baseline doing is, as it connotes, slow and minimal.

Having Positive Presumption Versus Being Unable to Have Hard Conversations

Everyone can benefit from learning the unique gifts that each Enneagram type naturally embodies. We face an inevitable hurdle when our capacity to appreciate these gifts is hindered by our own agendas. For example, we generally hold the elevated standards of Ones in high regard while we benefit from the fruits of their scrutiny—until the lens of improvement is placed on us. The transparency and direct honesty of Eights is often celebrated by those in need of a strong advocate, right up until the tough questions hit a little too close to home. The positive presumption that Nines offer to the rest of us similarly works in our favor, as long as we are the beneficiaries. It's refreshing to be on the receiving end of the benefit of the doubt, yet that enthusiasm slips away when Nines offer that benefit to someone we deem undeserving.

I was teaching a group of educators recently when I offered that a unifying factor for the gut-centered types (Eight, Nine, One) is that they all intuit dishonesty or lack of integrity. As Independent and Responsive types, Eights and Ones are more forthcoming in the ways that they solicit truthfulness from others. The withdrawing nature of Nines makes them much less obvious in this regard. You can imagine my delight when a Nine spoke up in her attempt to embrace this idea that "felt" like it hit home. Her response clarified just how much the positive presumption of Nines influences their responses in life. This Nine offered to the group, "I know when someone is stealing from me. When I let it happen, it is because I believe they must need it more than I do."

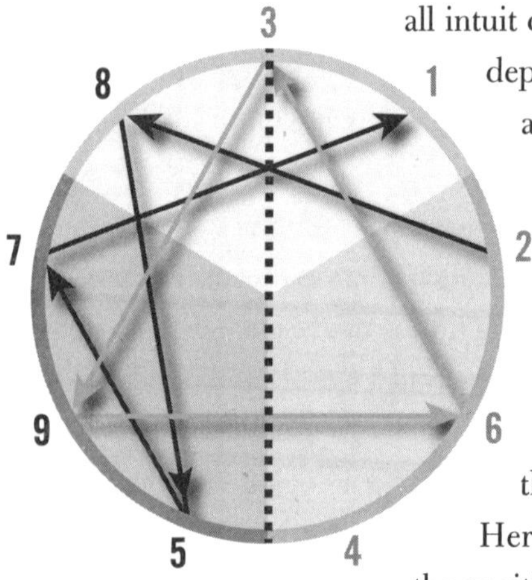

The unique combination of processing with objective reason and a natural deference to others makes Nines the most relatable objective type. Nines are one of only four types who bring logic and objective reason to work (left side of processing divide).

As the most relatable objective type, Nines are natural conduits for the five types who do not naturally draw from the Thinking Center at work. They uniquely possess an intuitive ability to represent and share objective reason in a way that can be embraced when emotions or subjective views govern thinking.

The truth is, Nines not only possess the ability to have hard conversations, they are the type most naturally equipped to deliver tough news in a way that can be accepted and understood by the recipient. My husband was the principal of a charter school for nearly a decade early in his career. In that role, it was his responsibility to terminate employees who were not fulfilling their commitments to the vision and mission of the school. Every terminated employee, to the person, thanked Billy as he ushered their exit. When the rest of us take the time to dig a bit deeper with Nines, we are likely to discover that the problem is not inability to have the hard conversation on the part of the Nine, but a vastly different timeline.

Nines are motivated to avoid, so it's easy for them to be comfortable with delayed action when others are distracted by emotional or dismissive reactions. Put simply, when we overreact, Nines are able to use our irrational responses to justify not addressing issues at work. When we adopt a fraction of the relational prudence that Nines utilize, it becomes incumbent upon Nines to overcome their own aversion to conflict and have the hard conversations.

Taking Time to Process Versus Being Unresponsive

Billy and I started dating in college. It was clear to me early in our relationship that he was bright. My competitive nature led me to a burning question that I was unable to ignore: which one of us was more intelligent? So, I did what any self-respecting young woman in my position would do—I suggested that we take an IQ test. I will not keep you in suspense. My Nine husband has a higher IQ than I do. It is important to remember, when considering the slow processing speed of Nines, that there is no direct correlation to a lack of intellect. In addition to ingrained wisdom and discernment, Nines process with thinking, making them intelligent by nature. However, their capacity for elevated reason is often overlooked in our fast-paced society because Nines are the slowest processors.

There are several factors contributing to the slow or delayed processing of Nines. Their internal reference point and orientation to time in the past support slow processing but do not directly contribute to it. Withdrawing Fives are also referenced internally and oriented toward the past and are arguably some of the fastest processors on the Enneagram. Fives do not share the Nine's motivating need to avoid, natural deference to others, or aversion to conflict. This unique combination of inherent traits acts as a regulator for Nines in all the ways that they engage with others.

Years ago, I worked with a ministry staff in a Chicago suburb led by a high-functioning Eight to explore the ways Enneagram type influenced communication on their team. I incorporate panels as much as possible when I teach because they are invaluable in their capacity to engage participants and show the universality of Enneagram wisdom. A panel question that consistently produces quality teaching points is this: What do you wish others on your team knew about you? To this day, I refer back to the answer offered by a young Nine panelist whenever I am consulting managers of Nines. He said, "When we are in staff meetings, it takes all the energy I have to keep up with the pace of conversation and rapid-fire questions and responses. To then raise my voice above the rest to offer my input or viewpoint seems literally impossible."

When I come across Nines who are older, more seasoned professionals, the delay still exists but the reasoning is a bit different. Many Nines tell me that they prefer to wait until the end of meetings to offer input, finding it more beneficial to defer to other voices in the room that might state the Nine's point more concisely or with better timing.

One of the quickest ways to lose a Nine to the abyss of slow processing is to give superfluous context. This is easier to avoid in email and requires more intentionality with in-person conversations. Remember that Nines have the least energy on the Enneagram and can feel immediately fatigued when they open a long-winded email. The motivating need to avoid bolsters the Nine's internal struggle against time monopolizing to trigger intuitive anger as soon as they click open. If you want a timely response from a Nine, send an email with minimally critical context and a clear question or action item.

We can all get lulled into over-speaking when we talk to Nines because they are so slow to respond. Nines are comfortable with the long pauses and silent stretches that make most types feel ill at ease. The longer the discussion, the greater the chance of the Nine dipping in and out of focus. Rather than staying in conversation with a Nine too long, filling the silence with noncritical information, choose brevity and be clear with your request for feedback, both in scope and turnaround time.

Getting Along with Others Versus Being a Pushover

I am often approached to identify the Enneagram type of someone I do not know and have not met. It is an inevitable byproduct of promoting understanding of others. When asked, I lead with the important disclosure that motivation is the unseen invariable that informs the behaviors observed by others and thus cannot be determined accurately without consulting the person in question. With that disclosure in place, if the description I am offered leads me to consider Nines, my go-to question is "Does everyone like this person?" While that question may sound trivial or overly general, it is the fastest way to weed out every other type (including Twos and Sevens).

The key to the universal affability of Nines lies in the reality that they are self-forgetting. Consider my husband's use of the glass idiom when describing our family unit: He acknowledges that our Enneagram Four son's glass is half empty and our Enneagram Seven son's glass is half full. He describes my Enneagram Eight glass as running over (thanks to natural intensity) and says that, as a self-forgetting Nine, he lost his glass months ago but he's fine as long as the three of us have ours. Self-forgetting tends to imply that Nines know what they want and choose to forget that for the sake of what others want. The truth is that what Nines want is rarely clear-cut. Because it is easier for Nines to identify what they don't want over what they do, going along with others' agendas does not feel like a sacrifice for the Nine. The decisiveness of others alleviates the pressure that Nines constantly feel to have an opinion when they are the least opinionated type.

This is a space where a Nine with a strong Eight wing will show up differently from other Nines, especially in a work setting. I often refer to the Nine-wing-Eight type as "spicy Nines" because they tend to pop up sporadically with a strong opinion and will be uncharacteristically aggressive with their delivery of that opinion. (See Appendix A for information on wings.)

Integrity is a common thread in discussing Nines, especially when you examine their type through the lens of its dual meaning: moral uprightness and the state of being whole and undivided. While Nines are hardwired to withdraw from conflict that directly involves them, they are more confident and assertive in their attempts to harmonize conflict outside of them. Not only do they get along well with the rest of us, they often take it upon themselves to guide us to see the value in getting along with each other. Anyone who mistakenly views Nines as an easy mark will find themselves losing doubly. First, when their self-serving plan is inevitably stalled by the silent and unyielding stubbornness of the Nine (who will not act in a manner that is untoward) and second, when the Nine utilizes patience and objective reason to unify others on a path that is both right and good for all. Other types can benefit from actively seeking input from self-forgetting Nines, who process with objective reason and have no personal agenda.

Not Voicing Disagreement Versus Being Passive-Aggressive

It is limiting and confusing to refer to Nines as passive-aggressive. Honoring the consistent exception of the rare and sudden rearing up that Nines with an Eight wing display, they are undoubtedly the least aggressive of all the types. If Nines engage in passive-aggressive behavior, it is likely during stress when Nines intuitively draw behaviors from Six. Of all types, Sixes are the most clearly passive-aggressive in their outward attempts to control their environments. As mentioned in part one, the unrelenting immobility of Nines is a reflection of passive anger. An angry Nine will not be moved to act regardless of the external forces applied.

The unique combination of an internal reference point and solitary doing fuels the Nine's behavior that others justifiably misinterpret as passive-aggressive defiance. Members of the Solitary Stance (Fours, Fives, and Nines) all have an internal reference point, but Fours are responsive doers (secure line to One), and Fives are independent doers (secure line to Eight), which means that the doing of Fours and Fives is transparent. As solitary doers, the actions of Nines are not transparent, so it does not occur to them to share with the rest of us their own plan of action or their aversion to someone else's plan of action.

Nines arguably live most comfortably in the gray area. This comfort reveals itself consistently in their default to an omission bias—the tendency to evaluate perceived harm through passive omission as a morally higher ground compared to actively causing harm through commission. The Nine's ability to see both sides does not preclude them from experiencing disagreement. Their disinclination toward conflict causes them to refrain from voicing disagreement. In other words, a Nine who disagrees with you rarely vocalizes that disagreement while simultaneously being careful to avoid vocalizing agreement. Others walk away from interactions with Nines feeling confident that the agreeable Nine shares their viewpoint while the Nine walks away from that same interaction justifying their omission by convincing themselves that their disagreement does not matter enough to share with others. The Nine slips comfortably back into solitary doing, trusting the natural buffer of time to lull others into the complacency of their perceived compliance.

The key to bypassing this subtle song and dance that inevitably leaves others confused and frustrated days, weeks, and months after their initial exchange with Nines is to again lean into the Nine's integrity. If you want input from a Nine, ask them directly for that input and then listen without interrupting. A Nine will not lie to you, and voicing disagreement will usually include a meandering explanation that honors your point of view well before landing on their own. Repeated interruptions do nothing but justify the Nine's inclination to defer through silence: "Why ask for my opinion if you are not willing to give me the time and space to express it?"

Nines intuitively use omission to play the long game, and others' preoccupation with the swift attainment of their own agendas allows Nines to play that game successfully time and again.

Finding Satisfaction in Simple Tasks Versus Procrastinating

In addition to baseline doing, my Nine husband routinely acknowledges his intuitive default to a doing "on-ramp." He observes that most types, especially those who process with doing (Eights, Ones, and Threes) can jump into an arduous task with little to no preparation. Nines, however, need an on-ramp built into their to-do list. If he has a big project looming at work, Billy will arrive at his office and focus his energy on smaller, less pressing tasks like answering emails, organizing his desk, or checking in on students.

No task is too simple or menial in a Nine's purview. Our culture has become so accustomed to recognizing feats in our day-to-day lives that we have lost our collective appreciation for those who find satisfaction in the mundane. Our sons have played a myriad of sports over the years, and we do not leave a practice or competition venue without Billy picking up trash that others have haphazardly left in our path to the car. When our large extended family comes together to celebrate birthdays and holidays, Billy routinely takes it upon himself to do the dishes and pick up behind the children.

Enneagram wisdom shows each of us two sides to the coin that is the gift and burden of our unique motivations. On one hand, finding pleasure in completing the simplest of tasks is a true reflection of the humble servant heart of Nines. On the other hand, processing with objective reason means that Nines will always be able to come up with a justifiable excuse to delay doing whatever they keep putting off. When I consult Nines in a business environment, my consistent challenge to them is to make a weekly habit of completing the task that they are avoiding on their to-do list. This task is rarely daunting and serves as a reminder to Nines that their intuitive stubbornness often extends to their own agendas. Alternatively, the gratification they feel from completing simple tasks will only be amplified when Nines knock out something they have been circumventing.

Others must remember that Nines are not naturally equipped with the ability to prioritize. When teaching Nines, my mom used to offer the visual that my Nine father could pick up a stack of note cards and write each task on his to-do list on individual note cards before laying them out on a table. She would then relate that my dad could walk up to that table and, as a Nine, have no internal sense of which card to pick up first. Billy heard her teaching that early in our relationship and added that he might as well turn the note cards face down on the table—that is what it's like for a Nine faced with prioritizing any to-do list. Tasks will be completed, but there is no discernable order.

Seeing Multiple Sides Versus Being Indecisive

It is easy to highlight the yin and yang (opposite but complementary) motivations of Eights and Nines.

The complementary antonyms that characterize types Eight and Nine are numerous: loud and quiet, most energy and least energy, aggressive and passive, impatient and patient, reactive and nonreactive, to name a few. Having Nines in my life (father, sister, husband) means that I have had nearly five decades to navigate these opposing characteristics with people who are in my inner circle. In all of that time, decisive and indecisive has yet to be a reality.

Eights are the most decisive type, without question. Decisiveness is a defining trait of Eights that often leads people who have mistyped as Eights—and there are so many—to dive deeper into exploring their true type. Being gut-centered certainly contributes to the decisiveness of Eights, which means Ones also experience that influence when making decisions. The instinctive decidedness of Ones presents itself most clearly through black-and-white thinking. The only remaining gut-centered type is Nine. Nines don't stay in the Gut Center to process with action, instead shifting to the head center to process with logic and reason. We consistently miss the value that Nines bring as objective mediators either because we are too impatient to allow them to process at their speed or because we falsely regard them as indecisive.

An Enneagram Nine who is a leader in a global organization described a time in her life when her capacity for decision-making was stretched—during a kitchen remodel. She was acutely aware throughout that time that "decision fatigue" is real for Nines. If Nines are second guessing themselves, they are in stress and drawing from the low side behaviors of Six. Nines, at their core, are never anxious about decisions, they are fatigued by them. Nines are the only type to objectively see multiple sides to every decision, thus their hesitance to make decisions when surrounded by people who are emotionally invested or more decisive makes perfect sense.

So, how do you solicit input from Nines? Consider the following approaches. First, it is easier for Nines to recognize what they don't want than what they do. As a result, Nines are much more likely to offer substantive input when presented with options. If you want a Nine to make the decision, replace fill in the blank with multiple choice. Second, when you give Nines time to verbalize a plan of action, their productivity and timely follow-through increase exponentially. Nines believe that anyone can do what they do. Processing with objective reason and deferring to others fuel their tendency to fall back when others charge forward. In reality, Nines make tremendous mentors and should be sought after as such—not only at work, but in all walks of life.

TIPS FOR MANAGING OTHERS, AS A NINE

Be conscious of your motivation to avoid.

- The looming conflict that you create in your mind rarely actually exists and never carries the level of intensity that you perceive.
- Trust your gut. Don't let your positive presumption allow misbehavior to go unaddressed for too long. Your efforts to save one may lead to the loss of many.
- Your ability to have hard conversations that are mutually beneficial is unparalleled. Remember that what makes you uncomfortable doesn't bring discomfort to others.

Your input matters.

- Don't let your contemplation of a response become the response. In meetings, write down your input and don't check it off until you've verbalized it.
- People who report to you can learn a lot from you. Don't assume they will learn from watching. Offer feedback even when you feel it isn't necessary or wanted.
- Respond to others sooner than you want to. Be aware of your internal bias against the expectation of an immediate answer.

The latitude you seek can have unintended impact when offered to those who report to you.

- Threes, Sevens, and Eights are moving at warp speed compared to you and will not wait for your input. Be clear with expectations and non-negotiables early.
- Ones, Twos, and Sixes want your feedback consistently and often. Find time to listen and don't hesitate to set boundaries around the frequency and length of those conversations.
- Fours and Fives appreciate latitude but don't carry the internal balance that you do. Fours may require guidance in order to stand independent and be objective. Fives may require guidance in order to be responsive and relate appropriately to others.

TIPS FOR MANAGING A NINE

Don't assume you and the Nine are on the same page.

- Be clear with your timeline expectations and seek verbal or written confirmation on due dates.
- Break down requests into manageable chunks and let the Nine know what you think are the most important tasks on the list.
- Nines don't need a lot of context. Be concise and specific with what you are seeking from them (e.g., use "action item").

Latitude matters a lot to a Nine.

- Be conscious of the time, space, and quiet that you offer Nines to do their job well.
- Your timeline will always be shorter than the Nine's. If the due date is fluid, let them know. If it is not, let them know and remind them.
- Nines generally think very little of what they bring to the table. Offering latitude does not mean withholding praise and support. Acknowledge the ways the Nine contributes positively to the greater good.

Ask the Nine for input. You want it.

- Nines bring relatable objectivity to everything they encounter. Their point of view is extremely valuable and rarely offered unless they are asked for it.
- Don't put Nines on the spot. Let the Nine know in advance that you want their input and try to give them notice if you are going to ask for that input in a general meeting.
- When a Nine starts talking, listen. If they feel comfortable enough to offer their thoughts, let them do so without interrupting. Encourage them to verbalize a plan and offer to be an accountability partner.

ENNEAGRAM TWO

Personal connection is everything.

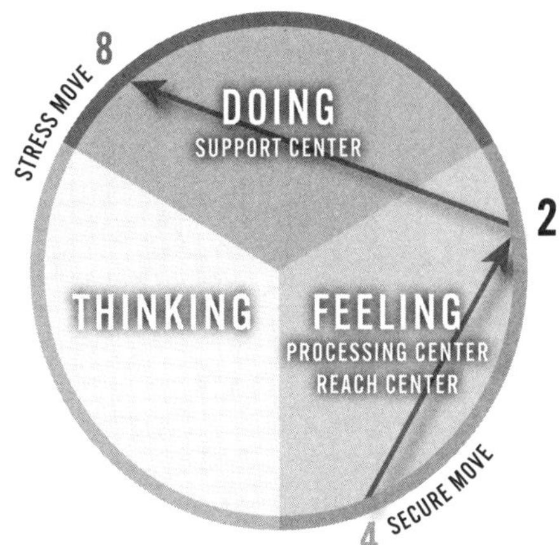

2s HOW TWOS VIEW THEMSELVES AT WORK	HOW OTHERS CAN VIEW TWOS AT WORK
I want to help.	You are always inserting yourself.
I want others to like me.	You are needy.
I prefer to discuss, in person.	You talk too much.
I am empathetic.	You are emotional.
I care for others' well-being.	You are easily distracted.
I value the opinions of others.	You are too trusting.
I am self-sacrificing	You are manipulative.

IF YOU ARE FAMILIAR WITH THE ENNEAGRAM, it is likely that you have encountered the work of my mother, Suzanne Stabile. It is impressive enough that she coauthored a book that has sold over one million copies worldwide prior to publishing two additional texts as a solo author. It is more impressive when you consider that her influential career as the Enneagram Godmother came in the second half of her life, following an equally illustrious first half. In the first half, Suzanne was named the first head women's basketball coach at Southern Methodist University after Title IX. Following my birth in 1978, she left coaching and utilized her BA in Social Work to start a shared housing program in Dallas that continues to this day to support at-risk single parent families and the growing elderly population. Not to mention the critical decade that she spent as a stay-at-home mom supporting the innumerable needs of a household of six in itinerant United Methodist ministry.

I believe her journey is a shining example of what it means to be an Enneagram Two. She has spent a lifetime making a difference in the lives of so many, yet the true scope of her impact is known by very few. This is largely due to the reality that Twos would be the last to share their resumes with the world. They live their lives recognizing and then meeting the needs of the countless individuals who cross their paths day after day. If need doesn't discriminate, neither does the Two. As the true empaths on the Enneagram, they see the rest of us in a way that we are often unable to see ourselves. They pick up our vulnerability as their own and then they do something about it. If there is a greater legacy than a life lived for the well-being of others, I'm not sure what it is.

Wanting to Help Versus Inserting Yourself

Twos are motivated by a need to be needed. Let's start here. The only two Enneagram types who have no direct line to the Thinking Center (Twos and Fours) are also the only two types whose motivating need requires someone else.

Ones have a motivating need to be perfect. While their external reference point means that they extend their lens of perfection outside of themselves, Ones don't need another person in order to achieve what motivates them. Threes certainly appreciate the external applause that the world offers to bolster their motivating need to succeed, but their competitive comparison fuels a very personal drive. With no direct line to the Feeling ("people") Center, the Five motivating need to perceive and the Seven motivating need to avoid pain are mutually achieved with the mind and, often to the chagrin of those closest to them, do not involve a reliance on others. While Sixes are natural community builders because they find safety in numbers, their motivating need to feel secure can only be realized internally. The Eight's motivating need to be against ironically involves everyone and no one at the same time, and Nines achieve their motivating need to avoid with ease when others are not involved. With no direct line to the Thinking Center, Twos and Fours are able to connect to action through Eight (Two stress line) and One (Four secure line) but their only other option is to stay in the human-centric center by sharing a line with each other. As a result, neither the Four's motivating need to be understood nor the Two's motivating need to be needed can be realized without other human beings.

Layer on top of this the reality that Twos feel what the rest of us are feeling long before they ever realize what they are feeling, and codependence in its simplest form begins. When your internal drive is to be needed by a world whose unique motivations are not inherently satisfied in connection to you, it is likely that the help you so generously and frequently offer is rarely actually solicited.

The Two's natural lack of personal boundaries is most recognizable in the spaces where unsolicited assistance takes on a life of its own. As the only Enneagram type hardwired to feel what others are feeling first and most, Twos cannot satisfy a need to be needed with people who are not suffering. This doesn't mean that Twos are unable to feel the joy of others, but it does speak to the truth that Twos are drawn intuitively to the rest of us when we are emotionally vulnerable and in need. In truth, we rarely have to tell a Two that we are not okay. Twos are able to sense that and then, as a Responsive type (One, Two, Six), feel compelled to do something about it.

In the chapter on Ones, I posited that the lines we share drive the unique ways that we think, feel, and do. While Ones are responsive doers and Sixes are responsive thinkers, Twos are responsive feelers. The line that Twos share with Eights means that both types are responsive feelers as well as independent doers. Independent doing, by its very nature, cannot be influenced. So, when a Two senses the unspoken or possibly unrealized needs of another, their swift and instinctive response with independent action can often be perceived by the recipient or casual observers as unrequested intercession.

A lifetime of being a Two and decades of intentional self-reflection have equipped my mother with hard-earned wisdom when it comes to her natural lack of personal boundaries. Part of the fruit of this wisdom lies in the three questions that she encourages all Twos to ask themselves before independently doing anything for someone else: (1) What is my agenda in extending myself for this person? (2) What, if anything, do I expect in return? and (3) Did this person ask for my help? These questions are helpful in a work environment because they break the loop that Twos unwittingly fall into of feeling what others feel and then doing something about that feeling. Feeling and doing, rinse and repeat. With an external reference point and no direct line to the Thinking Center, Twos must make a conscious effort to slow down and bring up productive thinking. Consistent utilization of these questions, when answered honestly, fosters that effort.

Wanting to Be Liked Versus Being Needy

It's a fascinating exercise for Eights to step into the mindset of Twos. Without intentionality, this can only happen, in part, when Eights are in a comfortably vulnerable space. Living forty-seven years in close relationship with a Two mother and a Nine father, who both naturally defer to others and jointly teach the importance of spiritual practices, suggests that I have traveled along my secure line to the Feeling Center more frequently than most Eights. And, while my hardwiring as a responsive feeler (secure line to Two) means that I am capable of empathy, which is arguably the most intimate way to connect with another person, I certainly do not need the other person to like me in the process.

> Enneagram understanding establishes that our intrinsic motivation cannot be altered. What changes with relative frequency is our behavior. Stress and secure lines and wings can all have a significant impact on behavior but are unable to alter motivation.

Consider that every Enneagram type, with the exception of Fives and Eights, is influenced in some way by a desire to be liked. This is largely due to the fact that every other type has the influence of the Feeling Center (Two, Three, Four) or Responsiveness (One, Two, Six) in their core type, their stress move, or both.

As the only dominant feeler and responsive type, the Two's eagerness to be liked is bone level. This explains why Twos uniquely depend on the rest of us to shape their opinion of themselves. Twos are simply unable to recognize their inherent value as something that is separate from our response to them and their ability to meet our needs.

The Two's external reference point exacerbates every basic drive. Constantly looking outside of yourself to satisfy internal desires can often be interpreted as "needy" by others. When Twos are not engaging in consistent solitude and introspection, their tendency to spiral into this perceived neediness increases exponentially. In these spaces, the Two's natural ability to read social cues is hindered by their unmet desire for personal connection and affirmation. Needy Twos generally take one of two paths: going after an unfamiliar person who might possibly hold the validation they seek or pulling in a familiar person by manifesting hurts or slights that don't exist. Since both paths are prevalent in most work environments, I encourage Twos to make a conscious effort to create space for solitude and introspection within their workdays.

My Nine husband says that Withdrawing types (Four, Five, Nine) need to "stop stopping" in order to be more balanced. Since the Doing Center is utilized least or last for these three types, that is sound advice. For the remaining six types, the balance we seek is impossible without stopping, and we all have a stress or secure line to Four, Five, or Nine for just that reason. Aside from stopping, Fours, Fives, and Nines personify the benefits of solitude and introspection—both inherent to having an internal reference point.

Twos are so tied to the cues they receive from others, bringing up thinking to develop personal boundaries is impossible until they spend consistent time drawing from Four to figure out what they feel, want, and need in the absence of others. The more that Twos are able to develop a sense of self in solitude, the less reliant they become on everyone else.

Preferring to Discuss Versus Talking Too Much

A natural function of utilizing the Thinking Center least or last means that members of the Responsive Stance (One, Two, Six) talk through their thinking or verbally process. Ones benefit from being the only member of this stance to process with doing, which supersedes their desire for connection with others. Thus, encountering "a talker" in any work environment likely means you are dealing with a Two or a Six, who both process with feeling and satisfy their desire to connect with the rest of us by engaging us in conversation.

> Because Sixes value information, verbal processing often satisfies their proclivity for needing to know why. Consequently, questions—both personal and professional—tend to surface most in conversations with Sixes. And when a Six's questions become repetitive in nature, it is an outward reflection of the second guessing that happens for this type who cannot help but see another angle.

Understandably, the anxiety that fuels the Heart Triad (Two, Three, Four) is most palpable with Twos, whose external reference point leads them to project their internal uneasiness outward. Simply put, Twos are generally uncomfortable with silence and are often the swiftest to fill silence with words . . . whether another person is present or not. Twos know this about themselves. I rarely encounter Twos who do not readily admit to talking out loud to themselves when no one else is around. During these encounters, I am intentional about not inflaming the shame that also fuels feeling-dominant types. I am quick to applaud the Two's self-awareness, and I encourage Twos to get into the habit of using those moments to organize their thoughts so they can simplify the delivery if and when they choose to share those thoughts with someone else.

Twos navigate life with an openness that draws the rest of us in and prompts us to share the rawest parts of ourselves with them. I have the great fortune of enjoying a long-term working relationship with a President and CEO who is a Two. The engaging vulnerability and genuine responsiveness with which he successfully leads his company invokes memories of the lifetime I have spent watching individuals share unsolicited and deeply personal information with my mother. Much of my respect for this President and CEO stems from years of observing his mindful discretion in conversation. He embodies a wisdom honed in the second third of life that will surely be influential as he enters the third third of life. This wisdom is possible for all Twos who spend decades realizing the impact of saying too much before learning the value of intentional prudence. For when Twos say too much, their verbal regurgitation comes from a deep spring of private vulnerabilities offloaded by others and unwittingly absorbed by the Two.

It would be lovely if we could fast-track the wisdom that comes with age. Since that is not possible, Twos would do well to organize their thoughts ahead of time when approaching important exchanges at work. If verbal processing represents a free-form essay approach to speaking, Twos are much more likely to garner the regard they seek from others with the focused brevity of bullet points. This technique makes an equal impact when applied to emails and verbal exchanges. When the exchange is verbal, Twos will find success carrying their bullet pointed thoughts into the conversation and sticking to that script. Going off script significantly increases the probability of saying too much.

Being Empathetic Versus Being Emotional

Continuing the thread of stance influence on the Centers of Intelligence, consider the feeling-dominant types (Two, Three, Four). As the primary type in the Heart Triad and Independent Stance, Threes are independent feelers. Just as the independent doing of Eights is transparent and cannot be influenced, the Three's instinctive ability to disconnect from negative emotion and project an emotion of their choosing creates a poignant visual for feeling that is visible to the outside world but not driven by the outside world. We have already established that Nines are solitary doers, which means that their actions are neither transparent nor influenceable. As the feeling-dominant type in the Solitary Stance, Fours are solitary feelers at their core. Whatever emotion Fours choose to share with the rest of us generally represents the tip of an iceberg of emotions that are constantly in flux—not transparent and not able to be influenced. Only when Fours shift from a self-focus to a focus on others in their stress move to Two does solitary feeling shift to responsive feeling.

As noted in part one, Twos are the quintessential responsive feelers or empaths. The only other responsive feelers on the Enneagram are Fours (stress line to Two) and Eights (secure line to Two). While every Enneagram type is capable of sympathy, Twos, Fours, and Eights are instinctively equipped for empathy. Add their transparency when it comes to feeling and they are widely viewed as the types who have the strongest emotions—often being regarded as "too much" when they share those emotions with others.

This regard can be especially burdensome for Twos in a work environment. As the only responsive feeler with an external reference point, Twos are easily distracted by the emotions of others. When Twos are anxious or in a lower functioning space, they will actively seek out coworkers who might be struggling as a way to fuel themselves with an emotional charge.

I remind Twos (and their loved ones) early and often that most of the emotions they take home at the end of a workday or work week were not the Two's emotions to begin with. Had that person not crossed the Two's path, the emotion they picked up would not even exist for the Two.

While it is imperative not to isolate gender differences when it comes to the Enneagram, sometimes these differences bear acknowledging. Wearing your heart on your sleeve as a female Two, Four, or Eight inevitably means tears. As an Eight whose internal drive requires replacing any vulnerable emotion with anger, I cry when I'm angry. In my particular work history, I have felt the most vulnerable when I was misunderstood in male-dominated environments. I can recall key moments when that vulnerability led to intense anger and that anger, in turn, led to tears. Jump into that female Eight nightmare with me. Just when I was gearing up to take on the injustice of not being treated equally to men, my responsive feeling led me to do a very "female" thing.

My own experience as a female who wanted to be taken seriously in those moments leads me to encourage restraint when I am consulting female Twos. Transparent emotion is so natural for them, and when you objectively consider that Ones are solitary feelers, Threes, Sixes, and Nines are independent feelers, and Fives and Sevens don't have a direct line to the Feeling Center, that adds up to a vast majority of people who are wired to be uneasy with a Two's open expression of feelings.

Caring for Others' Well-Being Versus Being Easily Distracted

Mercifully, I have very few regrets regarding my naturally blunt and direct delivery while teaching the Enneagram. Life presented me with hard-earned wisdom in my forties that I did not have on board when I began teaching this insightful tool in my early thirties. During those years of pre-earned wisdom, I had the opportunity to teach Enneagram stances to a large staff at a thriving United Methodist Church. At the end of a long and fruitful day of instruction, the Two who hired me shared with the room her struggle with self-care at work, citing the simple example of stepping outside for fresh air. She described that journey as nothing short of impossible because it meant walking by other staff members who would inevitably stop her with such frequency that she rarely made it to her destination before it was time to get back to work.

For context, this teaching opportunity came at the precise time when I was struggling to manage a Two at my own full-time job. The Two on my staff would spend no less than an hour every morning upon arrival and every afternoon after lunch walking around campus engaging others in conversation. Throw in an hour for lunch and a host of random errands on any given day, and she was out of the office as much as she was in the office. I realize now that my curt response was based on my personal experience. Even as I recount it here, I feel a familiar pang of regret. As soon as the Two on the UMC staff finished her reflection, I pounced. With a swiftness and dryness that bordered on condescension, I told the Two that I, like most people in the room, was able to step outside whenever I wanted without ever bearing the burden of delay that she described. All the understanding that I had spent a full day carefully sowing was undone in an instant.

Our exchange poignantly exemplifies the nonduality that Enneagram wisdom offers. While my delivery was deplorable, my message held the same validity that her reflection did.

If what you focus on determines what you miss, what are Twos missing when their focus is on others? That focus is both a superpower and a kryptonite. When mental energy is reserved for other people, the two things that would benefit Twos most—self-care and objective reason—are unattainable. When Twos honestly consider their return on investment with others, do the scales ever tip in their favor? How often is productivity sacrificed for relationship cultivation? Healthy and high-functioning workplaces require both.

Valuing the Opinions of Others Versus Being Too Trusting

While Twos, Fours, and Eights share responsive feeling and an inclination toward intense displays of emotion, there is a substantial divide when it comes to self-esteem. Eights arguably have the healthiest self-esteem, followed by Sevens and Threes. As established in part one, healthy self-esteem and high self-confidence are shared traits of the Independent Stance types who utilize the Feeling Center least or last, establishing a correlation between higher self-regard and lower reliance on the Feeling Center.

If the motivating needs of Twos and Fours cannot be realized without other human beings, it makes sense that both types would value the opinions of others and be acutely tuned in to the feedback they receive from others. With no direct connection (stress or secure line) to the Thinking Center and doing often bookended by a double connection to the Feeling Center, Twos and Fours are simply not equipped to objectively view themselves and what they offer to the world. Fours have the capacity to insulate themselves from overreliance on the opinions of others through an internal reference point and a natural disdain for social acceptance that requires loss of authentic self. Conversely, an external reference point and ingrained desire for social acceptance make Twos uniquely susceptible to connection with others at their own expense.

Despite having no connection through shared lines, triads, or stances, Twos, Sevens, and Nines can look very similar to a casual observer because all three types lean heavily into positively engaging the world around them (see the discussion on Harmonic Groups in the chapter on Threes). Sevens are known for their instinctual ability to reframe any negative into a positive. Being motivated to avoid pain while processing with thinking individually equips them to employ a future orientation to ignite delightful anticipation. Nines are known for their positive presumption. Shifting centers to process with preferred thinking individually equips them to utilize a natural deference to others to satisfy their motivating need to avoid.

While Twos are known for their positivity, processing with feeling means that their positive mindset comes at a personal cost. Reframing with thinking doesn't cost Sevens and Nines much because their optimism isn't reliant on others. For Twos to engage positivity, they must reframe people and relationships. This hardwiring inevitably makes Twos vulnerable to personal loss when others don't live up to the regard they so generously bestow on them.

Being Self-Sacrificing Versus Being Manipulative

If the three questions Twos should ask themselves before springing into action (What is my agenda in extending myself for this person? What, if anything, do I expect in return? Did this person ask for my help?) are useful for bringing up thinking, one could argue that Ones, Fours, and Sixes might also benefit from a similar line of questioning.

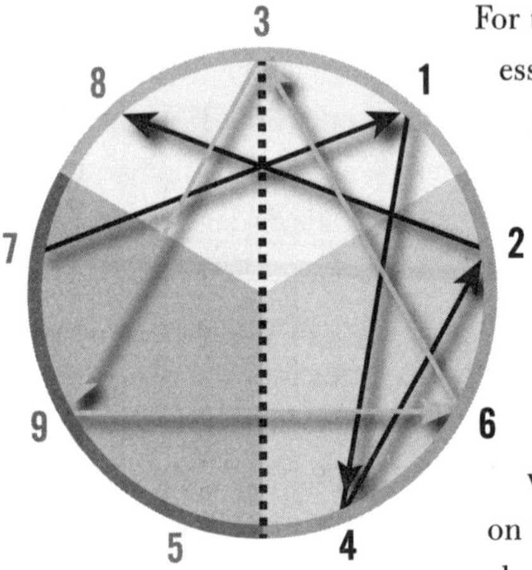

For those on the right side of the processing divide, subjective action is the natural consequence of utilizing the Feeling and Doing Centers in tandem. A commonality for these subjective doers that surfaces at work and at home is their experience with unmet expectations. While all types deal with unmet expectations, the types on the feeling side of the divide have unspoken or unrealized expectations specifically of other people. And when their expectations of others are not met, all four types respond emotionally.

Consider the fallibility of the Golden Rule. If treating others the way we want to be treated is human nature, we have all met disappointment when dealing with someone who is not motivated to see the world the way that we do. Twos are uniquely equipped to sense the needs of others. Their driving motivation is to meet those needs, and they often do that without being asked and at their own expense. The Two's personification of self-sacrifice stems from an inability to recognize and acknowledge their own desires. If manipulation stems from wanting something from someone else without directly stating what you want, Twos are naturally inclined to manipulate. Once Twos recognize that self-sacrifice and manipulation mutually stem from defaulting to others without realizing their own needs, they can begin to embrace the reality that neither course reflects healthy personal boundaries.

Utilizing Enneagram wisdom to achieve balance through self-examination is easier when we learn to recognize our own "red flags." One of the surest signals that Twos are steeped in feeling and far from employing objective reason is when they are martyring. This usually follows prolonged periods of doing for others when they are physically tired and emotionally overwhelmed. Consider the words of a brilliant pediatric anesthesiologist who shared some terrific insight about her experience as an Enneagram Two at work:

> All of this is even more pronounced when I pick up behaviors from Eight. I am a high-energy, proficient, efficient Two. So I am fixing things—people, relationships, situations—with alacrity. But then later . . . in the middle of the night . . . I'm awake thinking about who I might have bulldozed during the day. Because while I may not stop what I'm doing in the moment to attend to everyone's feelings, I definitely pick up on all of those feelings and, like a little emotional hoarder, pack them away.

Twos don't need to be in the high-stakes business of saving children's lives to reach this conclusion. An inevitable result of long workdays and hoarding emotions will be a tendency to martyr as they search for ways to express their own feelings surrounding unmet expectations. The more Twos can practice self-awareness in these moments, the easier it will become to choose an alternate path when the world does not reciprocate by sensing their needs.

TIPS FOR MANAGING OTHERS, AS A TWO

Be aware of the unspoken expectations that you place on others.

- Be clear and objective with your expectations of others. When you are on overload, watch the swift stress move to Eight. Your overreactions cost you the most.
- Giving low performers the benefit of the doubt reflects an expectation that being long-suffering will lead to improved performance. This is rarely the case.
- The people who report to you are not thinking of you with the frequency that you think of them. Your aim should be mutual respect, not mutual concern.

Your desire to be liked can present challenges in leadership.

- Be cautious of the ways you allow Threes, Sevens, and Eights to usurp authority. Self-confidence and independence should not supersede collaboration and consideration for others.
- Ones and Sixes share your responsiveness . . . and your desire for control. Ones focus on the task in order to achieve control. Sixes focus on soliciting information in order to achieve control. Make sure a clear chain of command is established and reviewed.
- Fours, Fives, and Nines need autonomy and latitude. Your desire for connection interferes with both. Be aware of the times you engage for too long because you cannot get a read on them.

Censor your verbal processing.

- Avoid giving superfluous context when assigning action items.
- Be careful not to say too much. Filling silences with personal information can be misleading and costly.
- In emails and meetings, focus on bullet points. Process and simplify your thoughts ahead of time and stick to the script.

TIPS FOR MANAGING A TWO

Twos need affirmation and that includes connection.

- When you are not okay, honor the Two's emotional intelligence by being honest about it.
- One of the best ways to show appreciation for a Two's efforts is individualized attention. Their focus is on you. So they feel valued when you pick up on the little things that reveal a focus on them.
- Allow the Two agreed upon time and space to verbally process and then actively listen.

The empathy that Twos bring to work is a gift to be used and not abused.

- Twos can tell you how your message is landing on others. That shouldn't mean they bear the responsibility of redelivering your message.
- Just because Twos are feeling what you are feeling, doesn't mean they should know what you know. Censor what you say in moments of shared vulnerability.
- Feeling is subjective. Don't be too quick to react to the feelings that a Two is sharing. Ask questions that require the Two to engage objective reason.

Twos don't have healthy personal boundaries. Sometimes those have to come from you.

- Consider your timing and the degree of priority when you ask Twos for anything. They will take on more than they should in their desire to be indispensable.
- Advocate for them and redirect tasks if higher ranking team members are taking advantage of the Two's inability to say no.
- If physical presence (in the office, at a workstation, etc.) matters to you, set a clear expectation for what that looks like early and often. Your idea of a productive workday will never include the magnitude of personal connection ingrained in a Two's vision of that same day.

ENNEAGRAM FOUR

Are you fulfilling your purpose?

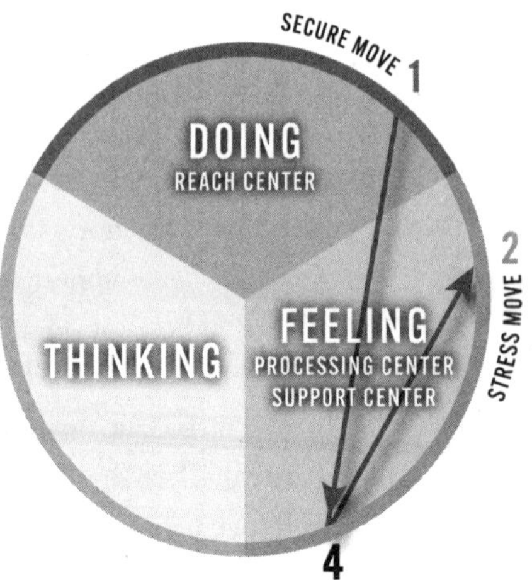

4s HOW FOURS VIEW THEMSELVES AT WORK	HOW OTHERS CAN VIEW FOURS AT WORK
I am perceptive.	You are overly sensitive.
I am passionate.	You are dramatic.
I appreciate authenticity.	You require too much.
I am reflective.	You are disengaged.
I am self-aware.	You are self-absorbed.
I am conscientious.	You are dissatisfied.
I am creative.	You are inconsistent.

FOURS ARE WIDELY (AND ACCURATELY) REGARDED as the most complex type on the Enneagram. Consider the subjective nature of the Feeling Center of Intelligence and the reality that Fours are the only type to employ feeling twice before doing because they have no direct line to the Thinking Center. If objective reason is a stretch for Fours, applying objective reason to quantifiably categorize them in any way would be an equal stretch. For all of their individual complexity, it makes sense that their driving motivation is to be understood.

Unlike Twos and Threes—who join Fours in the Heart Triad to utilize feeling first—or Sixes—who meet Twos and Fours to process with feeling—Fours are the only Feeling Center type with an internal reference point and the only Solitary type (Four, Five, Nine) to process with feeling. Fours stand alone as they approach the world with introspection on their own emotions and subjective views before shifting their focus outward to others' emotions and subjective views (stress line to Two).

Raising a Four child sparked an acknowledgment of and sincere appreciation for the lifelong journey that Fours traverse to discover and fulfill their true purpose. Because of their undeviating occupation of the Feeling Center, this purpose inevitably involves people. Regardless of the careers they choose, relationships matter deeply to Fours. Their penchant for uniqueness equips them to perceive and cultivate what is remarkable in others. The complex reality is that while we all benefit from their tireless devotion to the pursuit of meaning, Fours are tragically unmindful of their own remarkability. This reality inspires me to depart from the standard I have set in previous chapters and use the following pages to name the Fours who have uniquely enriched my own life.

Being Perceptive Versus Being Overly Sensitive

Acknowledging that there are fewer Fours and Eights than any other type would be the first of a surprisingly long list of parallels between Fours, whose driving motivation is to be understood, and Eights, who are generally the most misunderstood. Both are deeply passionate and intense, and their ability to detect disingenuousness is unmatched. While mistyping as an Eight is exceedingly more common than mistyping as a Four, Eights and Fours are the least susceptible to mistyping themselves.

For all that they share, Fours are the only type on the Enneagram for whom feeling supports feeling (stress line to Two), while Eights draw from feeling (secure line to Two) least or last. Processing with feeling means that Fours have the same capacity for heightened people awareness that Twos have while the Four's internal reference point endows them with a deep knowledge of self that is the Two's aim (secure line to Four). Given the attuned gift of perceptiveness that accompanies such hardwiring, Fours are uniquely equipped to offer the rest of us the understanding that they crave and rarely receive.

David, Enneagram Four

I met David in 2005 when he and I were hired as head coaches and administrators to build a Catholic high school. I remember being struck both by his perceptiveness and his tendency to downplay his sensitivity. Amid my own journey navigating life as a female Eight who had been repeatedly scorned for the same approach that garnered praise for male Eights, I was now working closely with a male Four who did not fit societal gender stereotypes either. Differing motivating needs and fueling emotions led us to respond to the narrow-minded predispositions of others in distinct ways. Shame colored David's desire to be understood while anger effortlessly fueled my desire to be against. In my worst moments, it did not take much for me to dismiss his diplomacy as weakness. The truth is, in the fifteen years that we worked together, the strength of David's sensitivity toward others (including myself) consistently and graciously truncated my numerous and potentially problematic vexations.

I am grateful to David for modeling the beautiful complexity that accompanies being a male Four. He and my husband Billy committed to coaching our son Will's select baseball team from grades four through eight, and the Enneagram was a consistent topic of conversation in the meaningful downtime that surrounded practices and games. Our family fondly regards those seasons as being deeply formative for Will and our ability to understand him.

Being Passionate Versus Being Dramatic

One of the driving reasons behind the unique complexity of Fours is the understanding that their emotions fluctuate at an exceedingly more rapid pace than other types. Exacerbating this constant movement is the reality that Fours are wired to feel every emotion deeply and thus begin curating the distinctive trove of methods they use to intensify feelings from a very young age.

Their internal reference point and feeling dominance make Fours one of the most self-referencing types. Self-focus is compounded by the intuitive sense that they are missing something that everyone else has. Add that their only optional focus shift is external (lines to One and Two), and you get "push-pull," a label that describes the tactics Fours use to reconcile a perceived internal void with an external solution. Fours are continuously seeking what they believe will make them feel complete. This search tends to land on a kaleidoscope of people, places, and things. Once a Four has identified what they believe might complete them, they pull. Pulling can vary from elevated interest to borderline infatuation. As the object of interest gets closer, Fours inevitably find flaws, and rejection, or push, follows. Once the rejected object is ignored by the Four or moves away on its own, renewed desire surfaces and the Four begins to pull again.

Remember that Twos and Fours are the only types whose motivating needs require other people. When Fours draw from Two and their focus shifts from self to others, emotional fluctuations shift from internal to external and require response from others. This is a messy, unpredictable space for Fours, who can be viewed as dramatic. In their efforts to solicit understanding in personal and professional relationships, push-pull intensifies until a desired reaction is received. Drastic pushes inevitably elicit reactions that the Four uses to justify perceived abandonment. Follow up pulls cloaked in passionate rhetoric fuel a self-fulfilling prophecy of being too much for others.

A good practice for Fours is to be mindful of the ways they create unnecessary drama in their efforts to make the outside world align with their fluctuating internal world. This is a subconscious move (more often than not) and can be tempered with body movement. When Fours begin to preplan elaborate withdrawals so they may savor a blossoming melancholic mood, opting for something active like exercise or an act of service for someone else presents a healthier way to channel emotional energy. Making physical activity a consistent practice will mitigate those deep plunges into emotion that leave others reeling.

When Fours choose not to retreat further into their own world, the responsiveness that connection to One and Two offers Fours channels passion into benevolence. Their energy transfers from the anxiety of satisfying shifting personal impulses to a genuine desire to serve others. When Fours apply the richness of interior depth to producing and accomplishing for the greater good, employers, peers, and clients benefit considerably.

Elizabeth, Enneagram Four

My relationship with Elizabeth was cultivated during a delightful span of time in my mid-thirties when I accompanied my mom on several trips to teach budding groups of Enneagram enthusiasts in Jackson, Mississippi, and Austin, Texas. Born and raised in Jackson, Elizabeth honed her exceptional artistic talents in New York and Paris before settling in Austin. Her passionate panache illuminated the value of visceral experience each and every time she so generously opened her kitchen and her home. Whether we were with her mother in Jackson or her family and friends in Austin, the expansive beauty of an uninhibited soul emanated from Elizabeth's painting, cooking, and conversing. She is the first female in my life to meet my intensity in a way that I could respect and learn from.

I am grateful to Elizabeth for being my friend. If I was to encapsulate her influence on my life in her language, I might say that she sparked my awareness of the divine feminine. Since I am unable to authentically deviate too far from the practicality of my own "feeling last" language, I'll say that she taught me the importance of nurturing relationships with other women, a gift that continues to serve me well personally and professionally.

Appreciating Authenticity Versus Requiring Too Much

As someone who appreciates authenticity, it never really occurred to me that possessing such a trait could be burdensome for others. This is largely due to the reality that I am autonomous in my appreciation and thus am able to stand independent from inauthenticity. Though Fours possess a natural gift for connecting with others in a way that elicits depth, a compulsory desire for authenticity can be disconcerting for other types.

As the other two gut-centered types, an intuitive drive toward integrity equips Nines and Ones to show up authentically when they engage Fours. However, the Nine's genuine struggle to meet a Four's intensity and the One's preoccupation with productivity create natural barriers for communicating with Fours at work.

Authenticity can be daunting if you don't know or like who you are. This concept has long separated Twos and Threes from Fours in the Heart Triad. The uneasiness within that prompts Fours to loathe social conformity triggers the opposite reaction in Twos and Threes, who tend to over-rely on the comfort that adjusting to social norms provides them.

I am continually intrigued by Enneagram influencers who mistype themselves. Likely stemming from the influence of instinctual self-deceit, the majority seem to be Threes who identify as Twos or Fours. The observable trait in Fours of embracing authenticity in defiance of conformity calls to mind one such personality who publicly claims to be a Four and repeatedly uses airtime to convince self-typed Threes that they are Fours. While the Four's private plight of being one of the unrecognized few makes them the least predisposed to this manner of coercion, it neatly fits a Three's driving need to be recognized among many.

Although an internal reference point wires Fives toward the same introspection that drives Fours, the natural chasm that exists between Fives and Sevens, who have no connection to the Feeling Center, and Fours, who have no connection to the Thinking Center, also colors their widely different interpretations of what it means to be authentic. Fives and Sevens appreciate the integrity of data while the Four's chief concern is the integrity of emotion.

Which leaves us to consider Sixes, who arguably feel stronger than their Head Triad counterparts about the legitimacy of data but ironically mistype as Fours more than any other type is prone to. This reality speaks volumes about the impact of processing centers in Enneagram understanding. The Six's tendency to mistype as every number will be discussed in the chapter on Sixes. While both Fours and Sixes recognize internal anxiety and process with feeling, a defining characteristic of each that settles in stark contrast to one another is that Sixes talk and Fours listen.

George, Enneagram Four

What struck me most about George when I met him over a decade ago was his sincere interest in listening to the stories that make up people's lives. A self-proclaimed lifetime learner in his seventies, George is easing into retirement and fills the growing spaces once reserved for treating patients as a geriatric internist with a keen appreciation for books, exploratory conversations, and the Enneagram. He carries himself with an aura of genuineness that invites others to unburden themselves from the trappings of curated image before engaging him.

I am grateful to George for the way he sees me and shares that view with others. George serves on the board for a community that hosted me for a weekend of Enneagram teaching years ago. When he informed me that he was going to give my introduction, I told him what I tell everyone who hires me and prepares my intro: "All the pertinent points of my bio will be covered while I teach, so use my intro to share how the Enneagram has impacted your life, specifically." While I'm certain that George understood the assignment, he focused his opening remarks on the personally enriching impact of getting to know me. To tell you that this hardened, misunderstood female Eight was moved would be an understatement. In the span of five minutes, George singlehandedly shifted the well-worn public lens of intimidation to intrigue. To this day, returning to his learning community feels much like going home.

Being Reflective Versus Being Disengaged

Nearly a half century of navigating the world as a female Eight has equipped me with a well-honed sense of being on the outside looking in. For years, I could rattle off, with ease, all the ways I didn't fit the collective wholes that surrounded me. Once I began to view my life through the lens of the Enneagram, I gained two powerful realizations regarding my perceived predicament. First, being an intuitive Eight with a support line to Five means that my reactions to not fitting in come from my gut and my mind, but never from my heart. Acting like or thinking about being an outsider is vastly different from feeling like one. Second, the common thread that exists for every type within stances does not extend to Fours, who feel like outsiders.

Consider the Independent Stance. Threes shift away from the Feeling Center to process with doing. Sevens support thinking with doing (line to One) and Eights support doing with thinking (line to Five). The common thread of doing means that we collectively have the most energy for action. For members of the Responsive Stance, Ones support doing with feeling (line to Four), Twos support feeling with doing (line to Eight), and Sixes shift away from the Thinking Center to process with feeling. The common thread of feeling means that these types collectively consider others as they respond to the world. There is a common thread in the Solitary Stance. The Nine's shift away from the Doing Center to process with thinking aligns them with Fives who support thinking with more thinking (line to Seven). This leaves Fours to stand alone with introspection that is both tethered to and supported by feeling (line to Two).

Fours must feel like they can't win at times, no matter how they engage others. When they shift their internal focus outward to convey their reflections, they can be received as overly sensitive or dramatic. When they read how they are coming across or are mindful of internal fluctuations and choose to minimize what they share with others, they can be chastised for being too withdrawn. When our son Will was entering his early teenage years, my husband Billy came up with a terrific metaphor for engaging Fours amid just such a palpable struggle. In Billy's language, Fours are on a roller coaster. If you are not a Four, you cannot get on the roller coaster with them. The sheer g-force of this roller coaster, with its twists and turns and loops would surely incite vertigo. The key is not getting on the roller coaster and not leaving the amusement park. Our tendency is to get on the roller coaster and get sick or leave the amusement park altogether. Both choices reinforce the Four's feeling that they do not fit with the rest of us. There is a third choice. Patiently waiting at the exit of the roller coaster is one of the best ways to honor the Fours who matter to us but may not be able to see it from the outside looking in.

Brehn, Enneagram Four

My guess is that not many people can say they were invited to be guests at the intimate nuptials of their local hangout's bartender. When the bartender is a beloved, salt of the earth Enneagram Nine in recovery who marries a reflective, force to be reckoned with Four in recovery and you share a mutual and deep respect for the wisdom of the Enneagram, that invite might be a foregone conclusion. It was initially at Brehn's request that her bartender boyfriend (at the time) introduced us. She was working at a no-cost recovery community for alcoholic women in Dallas and wondered if I might consider introducing the Enneagram to her staff. I wholeheartedly accepted, eager to pay forward the blessings that my family has experienced during my own brother's recovery journey.

> Regarding his recovery journey, my Enneagram Seven brother has often reflected that the Twelve Steps got him sober and Enneagram understanding keeps him sober.

I am grateful to Brehn for the myriad of ways that she enhances people's lives through her reflective nature. It has been such a gift for me to observe her in her element, guiding women who are struggling to piece back together lives that have been shattered by addiction. My *myriad* word choice is intentional, as Brehn's reflections are not limited to recovery. While she doesn't have the platform (yet) to win an Emmy, she rivals Andy Cohen in her nuanced musings on reality television, and her passionate pleas on behalf of shelter pets are the sole reason the perfect dog for our family was rescued days prior to being euthanized.

Self-Awareness Versus Self-Absorption

Regardless of religion, race, culture, or creed, solitude and introspection are cornerstones of a meaningful spiritual journey. Renowned philosopher Francis Bacon put humanity's inherent struggle with solitude into words centuries ago in his essay "Of Friendship": "Whosoever is delighted in solitude is either a wild beast or a god"—and members of the Solitary Stance (Fours, Fives, and Nines) are uniquely hardwired for it. If balance among the Centers of Intelligence requires self-understanding and self-understanding requires solitude and introspection, we all possess an instinctual trajectory toward the knowledge of self that awaits us through our connection to Four, Five, or Nine.

For most of us, withdrawing into solitude and introspection engages our Thinking Center. Since Fives and Nines process with thinking, objective reason is a natural result of slowing down and looking inward for them as well as Sevens and Eights (lines to Five) and Threes and Sixes (lines to Nine).

Fours are the only solitary type to process with feeling, making preoccupation with feelings and comparison to others an inevitable byproduct of solitude and introspection. Since Fours are naturally equipped with an internal reference point, preoccupation and comparison do not evoke the discomfort that they do for Ones and Twos (lines to Four), who possess an external reference point and draw from thinking least or last. Looking inward for Ones and Twos can be overwhelming—a principal reason both types tend to avoid it.

Extend this understanding to the reality that awareness of others requires drawing from the Feeling Center. Fours represent awareness of self that is tethered to awareness of others, laying the foundation for the envy so often associated with their type. While Ones, Twos, and Fours arguably struggle most with healthy self-esteem, solitude grounded in feeling equips these three types to elicit depth of emotion from others in profound and meaningful ways.

Will, Enneagram Four

I distinctly remember the first time I joined Will for lunch in elementary school. He was in first grade, and we had just moved him from the private Catholic school he attended in kindergarten to the public school near our home. As we settled into the organized routine of lunchtime, I was in awe of the way he engaged his classmates in conversation. I watched him endeavor to connect with each six-year-old at our table by asking thoughtful questions and tailoring insightful discussion points to the understandably rudimentary responses he received. Billy and I had acknowledged that Will is an old soul years prior. As soon as he was able to speak and express himself, he could do so effortlessly with adults. While I had approached the world similarly as a child, my fluid engagement with adults was grounded in thinking (as opposed to feeling) and became a tactic I employed to avoid the awkwardness I experienced trying to relate to children my age. Thus, it did not occur to me that the wisdom and maturity Will elevated to engage adults would also carry to the first-grade lunch table where he sincerely sought the relatedness that I evaded at his age.

Fast forward to Will's senior year in high school. The beneficence that exuded from an eighteen-year-old Enneagram Four—who had been raised in a family where his motivating need to be understood was met—prompted the production of *The White Rhino Documentary* ("white rhino" being a nickname earned playing on the offensive line). Two of Will's introspective football teammates (an Enneagram Five and Nine) spent hundreds of hours filming and producing "a little project made as an encouragement of and reflection on the impact someone's life can have on others."

I am grateful to Will for being my beacon, inclining me to meet him in feeling (joint lines to Two) from the moment he was born. His unflinching self-awareness, guileless humility, and pure tenderheartedness inspire me to authentically draw from the Feeling Center early and often. The honor of being his mother has been nothing short of transformative.

Being Conscientious Versus Being Dissatisfied

In the early stages of my working relationship with David, the aforementioned Four, I thought he was a One. Every single minute of his days was meticulously accounted for. He did not like any white space on his Google calendar and would create appointments for everything, including sleep. Then Will came along and I began to understand that Fours rely on established plans because that knowledge frees up the mental and emotional energy they instinctively require to manage fluctuating emotions. Since responsive doing is a secure move for Fours (line to One), they reflect much of the conscientiousness indicative of Ones when they are productively doing at work. The flip of this coin is that Fours can also reflect the dissatisfaction prevalent in Ones when subjective perfection is unattainable.

For all the parallels that can be drawn between Fours and Ones at work, two principal differences color their interactions with each other and with others. The first is processing centers. Ones process with doing. While they cannot help but see where improvement is needed, Ones are able to productively respond to their unique view with action and implementation. Fours process with feeling. They cannot help but see what is missing and are wired to respond to that unique view with emotional rumination. Simply put, Ones are actively working themselves out of resentment while Fours are more inclined to marinate in envy.

The second distinction is comfort with melancholy. Ones avoid melancholy. They utilize responsiveness and an external reference point to engage others and elevate doing. This helps Ones outrun their own despondency. Fours savor melancholy. They utilize solitary feeling and an internal reference point to withdraw from others. This results in Fours amplifying their desolation. While both want others to share their high standards for doing, the emotional responses that follow others' failure to meet their expectations reflect distinctly individual stress moves. When the One's standards are not met, their focus shifts inward to self (stress line to Four) and an internal flogging at the behest of their inner critic. When the Four's standards are not met, their focus shifts outward to others (stress line to Two), where dissatisfaction can take the form of intense and unforgiving judgment. Fours function well in professional environments when they employ heightened awareness around this intuitive move, as it can be costly to their working relationships. When Fours are intentional about moving beyond inevitable disappointment, there are tangible benefits to their vision of what's possible.

Alyssa, Enneagram Four

A beautiful gift of running a high school admissions office long enough to see alumni graduate from college and enter the workforce is having the privilege of employing the rock star student ambassador you were fortunate enough to mentor for years before hiring. Alyssa will likely carry the distinction of being the youngest Director of Admissions for years to come, a title she began earning in high school by conscientiously guiding her student peers on a recruitment leadership council that augmented the largest consecutive enrollment increases in school history and established recruitment protocols that have stood for over a decade.

I am grateful to Alyssa for her constancy. From the formative high school years that included caring for my boys and dog sitting when we traveled, through flourishing at an out-of-state university, joining forces with me to lead and grow her alma mater, and following a passion for teaching yoga philosophy and practices, our mutual affinity has remained intact. She will tell you that I am one of the few people in her life who understands her. My hope is that she is able to embrace all the ways that she has been one of those few people for me.

Creativity Versus Inconsistency

While it is a valuable practice within any system not to make sweeping generalizations about a specific type (remember human agency), creativity is a common thread for Fours. Our collective understanding of creativity rarely moves beyond the scope of being an artist. Not all Fours are in the creative arts and not all creative artists are Fours. That being said, Fours are creative by nature.

As members of the Independent Stance, Threes, Sevens, and Eights represent independent feeling, thinking, and doing, accordingly. Possessing the innate ability to stand independent from what is happening equips this stance to experience for themselves and offer to others the consistency that they value as they go through their days.

Similar to the solitude and introspection that is available to every type through their connection to Four, Five, or Nine, the ability to stand independent is possible for all types who have a connection to Three, Seven, or Eight. This means that every type has independence ingrained in them except Fours. Consider Twos, whose external reference point and lack of direct connection to the Thinking Center prompt them to struggle most with personal boundaries. When Twos can draw from the high side of Eight, they achieve consistency by independently setting and honoring unapologetic boundaries.

Understanding complex Fours involves taking in and absorbing the actuality that Fours must navigate life without access to a currency of consistency attainable by every other type. As a result, Fours are hardwired to take things personally. Fours (followed by Ones and Twos) can get derailed in a working environment by the unpredictability of what they take personally. This reality can be particularly stressful for the independent managers of these three types who crave consistency and reject emotion at work. Though managers may struggle with the inconsistency and emotion that subjective thought brings, this feeling is also, by its very nature, creative.

Cody, Enneagram Four

Cody's creative innovation has added substantial consequential value to my professional life for over a decade. When he was in high school (one year behind Alyssa), I tasked him to produce an annual video that encapsulated student life and would motivate students who had been accepted for admission to enroll. He did such an incomparable job that I hired him as a college student. When I left education to start my own consulting business, he was my first and only call to build my website and help create my brand.

I am grateful to Cody for his insight. I trust him to guide me into the creative spaces that my logical brain impedes, and I depend on him to illuminate the benefits of advancing technology that my advancing age obscures. His creative support of my vision for imparting Enneagram wisdom to others is deeply inspiring.

TIPS FOR MANAGING OTHERS, AS A FOUR

Be mindful of your innate inability to stand independent.

- You are hardwired to take everything personally. Before you react, audit your thought process for facts and observable truths.
- Comparison is a slippery slope for you. Practice catching yourself and redirecting your thinking early.
- Others will rarely align with the depth of your vision. Learn to temper your disappointment with gratitude.

While consistency is counter-intuitive for you, it is necessary in management.

- The consistency you offer Threes, Sevens, and Eights is far more important than the latitude you offer. They appreciate the latitude but need the consistency.
- Ones, Twos, and Sixes align with your passion for people, but elevate doing by being responsive. You will earn their trust with your actions, not your words.
- While Fives and Nines share your desire for latitude, too much is problematic. Consistent check-ins can be helpful for Nines who need to prioritize tasks and for Fives who benefit from increased social awareness.

Not everything has purpose and depth and meaning. Sometimes it's just work.

- Routine, though mundane, provides stability and promotes productivity.
- Those who report to you might share your sentiment but will never share your passion. That's not about you.
- Be aware of your tendency to sabotage when things are going well. Learn to appreciate the banal humdrum of quiet efficiency.

TIPS FOR MANAGING A FOUR

Don't get on the roller coaster.

- Fours cannot help but see what's missing. Catch yourself before you react to their reactions.
- Avoid engaging in on-the-spot conversations. When a Four wants to talk, ask them to schedule a meeting and send you a brief summary of what they want to discuss.
- Sometimes Fours need help getting out of their own way. Look for ways to engage them in activity or objective thought.

Structure matters. A lot.

- Oblige Fours the latitude to be fluctuating. For everything else, routine and order pave the way to productive doing.
- Be clear and detailed with your expectations. Fours can make nuance a ten-course meal.
- Fours need privacy. Build time and space into structure that allows them to withdraw in solitude.

The Four's motivating need is to be understood. Be intentional about your efforts to understand.

- Fours are comfortable with melancholy and distrust excessive positivity. Stop asking them what's wrong.
- Fours are searching for meaning and purpose and relatedness. Avoid being too transactional with your requests.
- Be consistent with your interactions. Keep coming back to the table to show them that you see them and you hear them.

ENNEAGRAM THREE

You see what I want you to see.

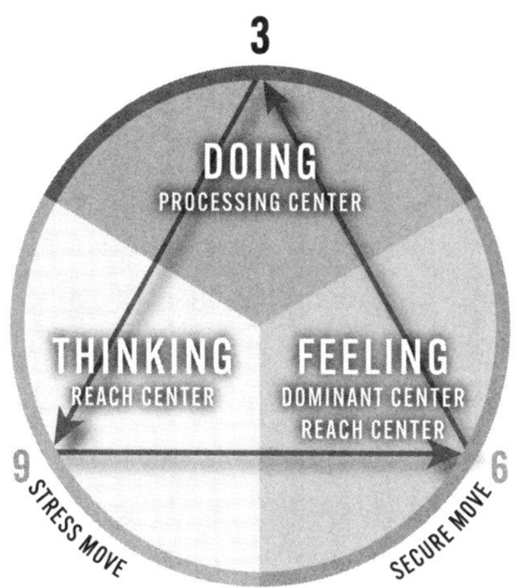

3s HOW THREES VIEW THEMSELVES AT WORK	HOW OTHERS CAN VIEW THREES AT WORK
I am adaptable.	You are disingenuous.
I am efficient.	You are careless.
I am driven.	You are overly ambitious.
I am personable.	You are impersonal.
I like to motivate others.	You are presumptuous.
I prefer to multitask.	You overreach.
I am competitive.	You are conceited.

CONSIDER THE REALIZATION of our intrinsic motivations as two sides of the same coin. One side engages the world and the other side prompts self-reflection. Some types are predisposed to focus outward while others intuitively lean inward. As the gut-centered type with an internal reference point, Nines are arguably motivated to be the most comfortable with honest self-examination. Conversely, fueling uneasiness within and external or independent reference points make it the most challenging for Twos and Threes to reflect internally for personal growth.

When assessing Threes as a type, the allegory "The Emperor's New Clothes" comes to mind. (Incidentally, I would not be surprised if an analysis of historical allegories, especially those meant to explain human nature, reveals consistent ties to the primary types—Three, Six, Nine. Being the center point of each triad prompts Threes, Sixes, and Nines to see themselves in other types, which may inhibit their ability to land confidently on type initially, but it certainly equips them to connect with the rest of us with relative ease.) Hans Christian Andersen's story, published in 1837, is based on a medieval Spanish tale written by Juan Manuel in the early 1300s and has been translated into more than one hundred languages, making it one of the most broadly recognized allegories in existence. It provides a terrific illustration for reflecting how difficult it must be for Threes to engage in self-examination when their hardwiring hinders it and their external world prevents it. If the emperor represents Threes, the townspeople represent a world that doesn't help others take an honest look at themselves. While Threes have the capacity to be the most influential of all types, the ironic flip of that coin is that they are the least equipped to do the internal work to ensure their impact is altruistic.

Adaptability Versus Disingenuousness

Threes are "Wizards of Oz" standing behind the velvet green curtain, controlling the levers that dictate what the rest of us see. As a passionate Eight who couldn't hide my emotions if I tried, I am keenly aware of the natural gift that Threes possess of being able to disconnect from negative emotion and project something more positive to others. Noting their home base in the Feeling (or people-centric) Center, the driving motivation that Threes have to be successful is intrinsically tied to people. I had a Three tell me one time, "If I cannot adapt to meet the expectation of the person in front of me, I feel like it's over—everything is on the line, every time." That reflection is a helpful reminder when working with Threes because it can sometimes feel like we are being played by the Three. It takes little effort to view the deceit that is a core struggle for Threes as their attempts to mislead us. Enneagram wisdom reveals that Threes are hardwired to adjust and adapt to others. Their chameleon nature is intrinsic and therefore not a conscious or calculated attempt to be disingenuous.

In truth, the Achilles' heel for Threes is not deceiving others but self-deceit. Their intuitive ability to adjust successfully to meet others' expectations without missing a step, combined with an ingrained hesitancy toward self-reflection, makes Threes the least inclined to be consistent with inner work. Add to that the reality that Threes are the only extrinsically motivated type in the Independent Stance (Three, Seven, Eight), and you get human beings with the power and confidence to mobilize masses toward a direction of their choosing . . . without an internal compass.

Being the primary type in the Heart Triad means that Threes possess the unique gifts for connecting with others that are inherent to Twos and Fours. For Twos and Fours, who process with feeling, relational connection is the end. For Threes, who process with doing, relational connection is the means to an end. While it can be jarring for others to realize the easy connection they made with a Three was multipurpose, making the leap to premeditated insincerity not only unfairly villainizes Threes, it gives them credit for thinking that was not actually employed.

My sincere appreciation for the unwavering logical sense revealed through this wisdom is bolstered by the reality that nowhere on the Enneagram does thinking support feeling or vice versa.

As members of the Independent Stance, Threes share the self-confidence, fast processing, and abundant energy for action that Sevens and Eights possess but propel forward without the objective reason naturally employed by Sevens and Eights. Sevens process with thinking and support thinking with doing (line to One). Eights process with doing and support doing with thinking (line to Five). As the primary type in the stance, Threes take in with feeling but shift to process with doing, thereby losing a support center. Like Nines with thinking and Sixes with feeling, the Three's shift to process with a center that is not their home base means that they stay in the Doing Center too long. This is where "fake it till you make it" resonates for Threes as they navigate the world.

While logic and objective reason await them in Nine (thinking), their avoidance of solitude and introspection leaves them frenetically shifting between action (doing) and engaging others (feeling), a poignant visual for the adaptability that Threes so effortlessly personify.

Efficiency Versus Carelessness

I love dealing with Threes when I am navigating the ins and outs of a new client relationship. They share my penchant for action and match my processing speed, uniquely equipping them to meet me in efficient decision-making at every turn. I don't believe I am exaggerating when I reflect that the time it takes me to accomplish anything with a Three takes two to ten times longer with any other type.

The Three's shift away from the Feeling Center to process with doing places them in a category with Eights and Ones that I have previously referred to as motors. Companies desiring long-term, sustainable growth will not achieve it without Eights, Ones, and Threes contributing to the decision-making process. As illustrated in the chapter on Eights, these motors rise to leadership positions more frequently than other types, and in leadership, a clear and consistent pattern of tension between resentful Ones and unwitting Threes typically rises.

In general, Eights and Ones work well together. As the two Gut Triad (Eight, Nine, One) types who process with doing, their standards for action are higher than most, making their thoroughness and practicality unifying. The Eight's independent reference point and supporting objective reason equip them to channel anger into action while remaining largely unmindful of those who meet their expectations and dismissive of those who don't. When Eights do manage to get crossways with a One and transparency does not bring resolution, the One can turn to any number of colleagues at the ready to privately dismantle the unaware Eight.

The One's external reference point and supporting emotion saddle them with the burden of turning anger inward while being cautiously cognizant of those who meet their expectations and judgmental of those who don't. Picture the scowl of an Enneagram One president and CEO when her Enneagram Three COO flashes his signature winning smile and tells their leadership team that he doesn't like the term "cut corners," preferring to use "round the edges" instead. Ones often find themselves elbow to elbow in leadership with Threes whose shift to process with a center that is not dominant precludes them from ever sharing the One's standards for doing. Adding salt to the inevitable wound is the Three's ability to get along well with others, leaving Ones without a willing advocate when they feel inclined to scrutinize the Three's actions.

The concept of Harmonic Groups is especially instructive for the positive-spin tendency of Threes. There are three Harmonic Groups as described by Don Richard Riso and Russ Hudson in their book *The Wisdom of the Enneagram*: the Positive Outlook Group, the Competency Group, and the Reactive Group. In the chapter on Twos, we looked at Twos through this lens. While Twos join Sevens and Nines in the Positive Outlook Group, their optimistic reframing comes at a personal cost that is ultimately unsustainable, causing Twos to shift from positive outlook to join their fellow feeling processors (Fours and Sixes) in the Reactive Group. Because they process with doing, Eights are not equipped to stay long in the Reactive Group, prompting their shift to join Ones and Fives in the Competency Group. While Threes start out in the Competency Group, they lack the task focus inherent to Ones and Fives (see Multitasking Versus Overreaching later in this chapter), causing them to shift from competency to join Sevens and Nines in the Positive Outlook Group. This intuitive shift from competency to positive outlook is generally marked by the Three's inclination toward positive spin.

Threes and their leaders should be cognizant of the Three's natural default to "smoke and mirrors." While taking the time to present others with a positive spin belies carelessness, Threes and their leaders can learn to use their shift from competency to positive outlook to slow down and regroup.

Being Driven Versus Being Overly Ambitious

Being mindful of the non-negotiables for each type as presented in part one, non-negotiables for Threes include the ability to disconnect from negative emotion and exhibit positivity while navigating life via personal and professional goals. Every type has the capacity to set goals for themselves. Only Threes use goals to pave their way through life.

While the successful application of Enneagram wisdom is largely immune to generational differences, there are times when generational differences exacerbate motivational differences in today's workforce. The same goal-focused drive that gifted Enneagram Three boomers and Gen Xers with promotions and perks, thanks to their ability to outlast or outmaneuver their equally hardworking counterparts, sets Enneagram Three millennials (also referred to as Generation Y) and Gen Zers apart as being particularly more entitled than their self-focused peers.

Threes are valuable employees regardless of generation because Threes, more than any other type, embrace the grind. This type is historically known for their ability to work long hours with very little down time. I had a millennial Three tell me recently that when he is not working and being active, his body physically hurts. The work–life balance of Enneagram Three baby boomers in their twenties would likely closely match Enneagram Threes in Generation Z. The intrinsic motivation of Threes has not changed, but societal reception of the characteristics that represent the Three's motivation has.

Consider two Threes who work for companies that are largely distinguishable based on average employee age. Company A is predominantly made up of baby boomers and Generations X and Y, with very few Gen Z employees. Company B is millennial heavy, followed by Gen Z, with no Gen X and no boomers on staff. These two Threes were born at the beginning of their respective generations, one in 1982 (Generation Y) and the other in 1998 (Generation Z). The millennial Three who works for Company A was promoted early and often, rising in the ranks to the well-earned position of COO while the Gen Z Three working for Company B has been repeatedly advised to be patient and pay her dues.

One could argue that the driving reason for their differing professional statuses is their sixteen-year age difference. This observation is certainly sound, and Enneagram understanding does not advocate for the blind promotion of twenty-somethings. Yet the observable truth is that sixteen years ago, the inherent ambition of the millennial Three was not rebuffed by the leadership of Company A. While boomers and Gen Xers differ on our interpretation of work–life balance, both generations historically reward the self-sufficiency that causes leadership-by-committee Generations Y and Z to raise an eyebrow. As the generational workforce balance continues to shift in the coming years, this reality will undoubtedly inhibit the professional growth of Threes, Fives, Sevens, and Eights more than any other type.

Being Personable Versus Being Impersonal

A helpful tool for understanding Threes taking in with the Feeling Center but not utilizing feeling to process is to visualize a Three who recognizes that a friend or colleague is struggling emotionally. Because the Three is feeling dominant and values interpersonal dynamics, they acknowledge the struggling individual to signal that they care. If the individual's response is to ask the Three to join them in processing burdensome emotions, the feeling least or last Three immediately looks for an out. If this Three can engage their processing center and *do* something to alleviate the struggle, they are all in, but to process emotions, the struggling individual would do better to consult a feeling processor (Two, Four, Six).

Having people awareness (feeling) as a filter and action and implementation (doing) as a processing center uniquely equips Threes with natural influence. Nowhere else is this influence more palpable than in churches. Most megachurch pastors likely are Threes. If you consider the documented rise in popularity of the megachurch in tandem with the aforementioned theory that a shifting generational workforce is less inclined to reward the Three's motivating need to succeed, more than ample evidence supports the argument that entrepreneurial Threes responded to waning popularity in the business sector by finding an untapped resource to make profitable.

Megachurches unabashedly represent the concept of being both personable and impersonal and don't pretend to be otherwise. Much like a marriage of convenience, the megachurch model offers the convenience of community . . . of intimacy . . . of a relationship with God—and the younger generations are responding en masse. Recent statistics show the average megachurch annual budget to exceed $5 million.

Threes, like their Seven and Eight counterparts in the feeling least or last Independent Stance, have good hearts. Feeling least or last is not a conscious choice for any of these three types, and they all seem to have a knack for getting in their own way in their rush to escape vulnerability. If one was to assign a tagline to the Independent Stance, it would likely be "It's not personal." This tagline generally extends to include Fives and Nines on the left of the processing divide who incorporate thinking into decision-making.

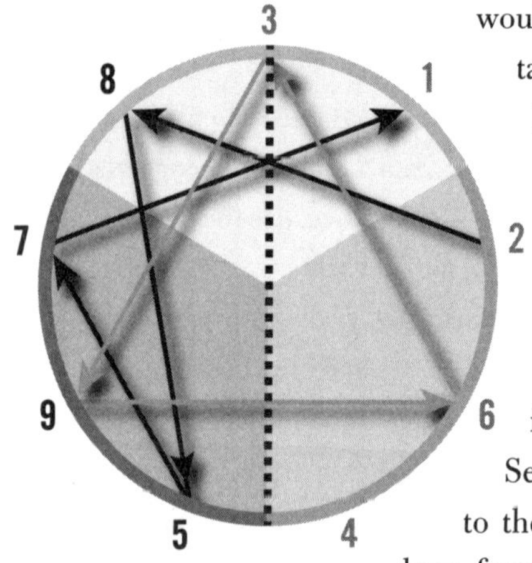

Narrowing the focus to Threes, Sevens, and Eights in the Independent Stance reveals helpful insight for working with Threes. Sevens, who have no connecting line to the Feeling Center, and Eights, who draw from thinking long before feeling, arguably have fewer expectations placed on them by the large population of types who incorporate feeling on the right of the divide. When Sevens and Eights live into "It's not personal," other types rarely bat an eye. When Threes live into the same familiar space, people who were personally engaged by the feeling-dominant Three can be harsh with their vindicated judgment.

Motivating Others Versus Being Presumptuous

For the primary types (Three, Six, Nine) who shift away from their dominant center to process with a preferred center, those two centers become inextricably tied to one another as the Three, Six, or Nine moves through life. Look at Nines who shift away from doing to process with thinking. Most of a Nine's mental energy encompasses what needs to be done. Acknowledging that thinking represents logic and objective reason, Nines are able to come up with a litany of logical reasons to delay doing. Sixes shift away from thinking to process with feeling. Sixes are notorious for engaging others through sharing personal information and looking to trusted advisors when a lack of transparency surrounding the distribution of data makes them feel uneasy. For Threes, who shift away from the Feeling Center to process with doing, action and implementation will inevitably involve people. Understanding that Threes are inherently collaborative doers makes it easy to see why they can be so influential as they engage the world.

While the word itself has a more negative connotation, many of the synonyms for *presumptuous*—bold, brazen, familiar—read much like a Three's bio. Since Threes are equipped with a sincere motivation to help others succeed, their perceived presumptuousness warrants a deeper dive.

I mentioned earlier that members of the Independent Stance (Three, Seven, Eight) tend to get in their own way. This is likely the case for all Enneagram types when we refuse the balance offered by elevating our repressed center. Take Ones, for example. As the only motor in the Responsive Stance, Ones have considerable capacity to substantially do for the greater good. When Ones refuse to consciously engage the flexibility that awaits them in thinking, their active fixation on the one right way to accomplish a task diminishes the greater good that prompted the One's involvement in the first place.

The Three's desire to motivate others comes from feeling, which is altruistic. But when the Three intuitively abandons feeling to double down on doing, their selfless intent is lost. Altruistic Threes have the unique ability to draw from feeling to inspire those around them. When doing overshadows feeling, the goal becomes bigger than the individual, and the Three's ability to inspire falls away while self-deception prohibits the Three from seeing that their influence has diminished.

Consider a Three from the advertising world who felt called to lead and grow a nonprofit that had long been connected to his church. His enthusiasm and vision were initially well received by stakeholders. In his first year, he inspired many with effective change management strategies. When a global pandemic brought his vision to a screeching halt, the Three was unable to rely on his marketing background for a silver lining and was unwilling to lean on the experience of his seasoned leadership team for a path forward. The Three spent the better part of his second and final year with the nonprofit sequestered in his office creating five-, ten-, and fifteen-year strategic plans while the constituents he had been motivated to lead forged through the pandemic without him.

Multitasking Versus Overreaching

Cognitive science has not wavered in its assertion that multitasking is significantly less effective than focusing on an individual task or monotasking. Diving further into the cognitive research reveals that our concept of multitasking is never actually achieved because the human brain must switch from task to task rather than handling tasks simultaneously. Taking this reality into consideration through the lens of the Enneagram presents primary types (Three, Six, Nine) with an added challenge because these three types are not equipped with an intuitive task focus.

The concept of "task focus" explains much about work behavior based on Enneagram type. While our reference point, determined by stance, does not change from being external (One, Two, Six), internal (Four, Five, Nine), or independent (Three, Seven, Eight), our *focus* can and does shift based on the lines that we share. Ones, Fives, and Eights are the three types whose hardwiring equips them with a natural task focus. In professional environments, they are generally highly regarded for their efficient and practical point of view as well as their ability to prioritize and delegate.

Twos, Sixes, and Nines begin with a focus on others. These three types typically find working with others to be the least challenging because they are uniquely equipped to defer to others. Twos defer to the feeling of others, Sixes defer to the thinking of others, and Nines defer to the doing of others. This natural ability to defer garners favor with peers and managers and solidifies the general consensus that Twos, Sixes, and Nines are easier to work with.

Threes, Fours, and Sevens start with a self-focus. Because these types know what they want from their environments, they tend to let personal preference drive decisions wherever they find themselves, and the workplace is no exception. Having a personal agenda that is top of mind drives decisiveness and equips these three types with a unique ability to influence others.

Eights are the only type with no line to Three, Four, or Seven, meaning they are the only type without an intuitive self-focus. This will come as no surprise to Eights but may be shocking to the masses who have grossly mistaken their self-confidence for self-aggrandizement. It does shed some light on why the Eight's decisiveness is so often misconstrued as having a personal agenda. Ones, Fives, and Sevens have no line to Two, Six, or Nine, and thus find it very difficult to defer to others. As the only independent thinkers on the Enneagram, engaging thinking that is transparent and not able to be influenced underscores the inability that Ones, Fives, and Sevens have to defer.

With no line to One, Five, or Eight, primary types (Three, Six, Nine) focus doubly on others and singularly on self but have no natural task focus. Threes make up for this by being a motor. Being the only doing processor without a task focus equips Threes to find the most success in multitasking. The downside to being a motor without a task focus is that Threes can struggle to stay in their lane, overstepping and overreaching, often without realizing it. Sixes make up for no task focus by being responsive. The downside to being in the Responsive Stance without a task focus is that Sixes can get overwhelmed as they take on more and more responsibility. If Nines are not engaged in doing that sparks their self-focus (line to Three), they are ill-equipped to overcome a lack of task focus (see the chapter on Nines). If there is an upside to this reality, Nines are not overreaching and do not get overwhelmed (see, also, the chapter on Nines).

Being Competitive Versus Being Conceited

As established in part one, Threes navigate life via competitive comparison. While fueling comparison can become competitive for the rest of the Heart Triad (Twos and Fours), it is always competitive for Threes. When you are hardwired to start with a focus on self and your motivating need to succeed is achieved through competitive comparison, it is understandable that others might interpret your actions as self-centered.

As I have already said, I have the most compassion for Ones. Based on personal experience and my disdain for inauthentic sentiment, my compassion for Threes takes the form of hard-earned magnanimity. Consider all the ways that Threes are naturally equipped to succeed through competitive comparison: They are the only type in the Heart Triad (Two, Three, Four) to process with action, they are the only primary type (Three, Six, Nine) to have high self-confidence and an independent reference point, they are the only doing processor (One, Three, Eight) able to disconnect from anger, they are the only independent type (Three, Seven, Eight) to have a naturally high EQ, and they are the only type in the Competency Group (One, Three, Five) able to shift to a positive outlook (see Efficiency Versus Carelessness earlier in this chapter).

As a fellow doing processor with an independent reference point, my consistent experience positively engaging Threes who are competitively comparing everywhere else is nothing short of effortless and comfortably copacetic. When Threes focus their competitive comparison on me (and most Eights, I imagine), things inevitably take a turn. While I am competitive, I am wholly internally motivated and thus not wired to compare. I have been absolutely blindsided more than once in my life by Threes when their competitive comparison prompted personal sabotage in their efforts to beat me at a game I did not even know I was playing.

Threes, at their best, have the capacity to truly inspire. The unequivocal prerequisite for being their best and most authentic selves requires the one thing that they are not inherently equipped for: honest self-examination. If knowing is half the battle, it certainly is the easy half. When Threes are able to consciously and consistently separate themselves from the intuitive trappings of self-deceit, altruistic intentions drive their focus on others, and Threes are able to authentically garner sustaining satisfaction from "we" wins as opposed to "me" wins.

TIPS FOR MANAGING OTHERS, AS A THREE

Say what you mean and mean what you say.

- People pleasing is in your DNA. Being liked won't serve you nearly as well as being respected.
- Be aware of your tendency to pass the buck. And then don't do it.
- The positive spin that might benefit the larger group can be detrimental to fellow leaders. Be conscious of what you withhold from whom.

Goal setting doesn't motivate anyone else like it motivates you.

- While you share a future orientation to time with Sevens and Eights, your goals are nontransferable. Try meeting them where you align in competitiveness instead.
- Ones, Twos, and Sixes are ruled by the immediate and are the least equipped to view work objectively. Future goals exacerbate present anxiety.
- Fours, Fives, and Nines don't like being told what to do or when to do it. Goals check both of those boxes.

Slow down . . . way down.

- Your lightning speed and ability to pivot are not reassuring for everyone. Meet people where they are when the message is important.
- Your poker face may conceal negative emotion. . . . It does not conceal when you check out of a conversation. Practice active listening.
- Work solitude and introspection into your daily routine. It's the only way to combat self-deceit.

TIPS FOR MANAGING A THREE

The ambition is real.

- Threes navigate life via goals. Don't mistake drive for disrespect or insubordination.
- If you give a Three a timeline for promotion, be ready to be accountable for every step.
- Titles go a long way and don't cost much.

Confidence and fast processing are not substitutes for

- attention to detail. Threes bring feeling values to process with doing. If "good enough" is not enough for you, establish that early and often and be specific with your feedback.
- thorough planning. Threes do not have a natural task focus. You will have to guide them to prioritize walking a path through to the end before setting an idea in motion.
- logic. Threes are generally convinced that they employ logic without slowing down and being intentional about it. They don't.

Learn to read the positive spin and watch for smoke and mirrors.

- Threes are masters at the art of misdirection. Encourage Threes to report what isn't working along with everything that is.
- A frenetic Three is a Three in trouble. Make sure they know they can come to you with anything. You will need to incorporate measures for slowing down to keep the Three from spinning out of control.
- Don't allow scapegoats. Responsibility must be taught and modeled.

ENNEAGRAM FIVE

Work is not fatiguing . . . people are.

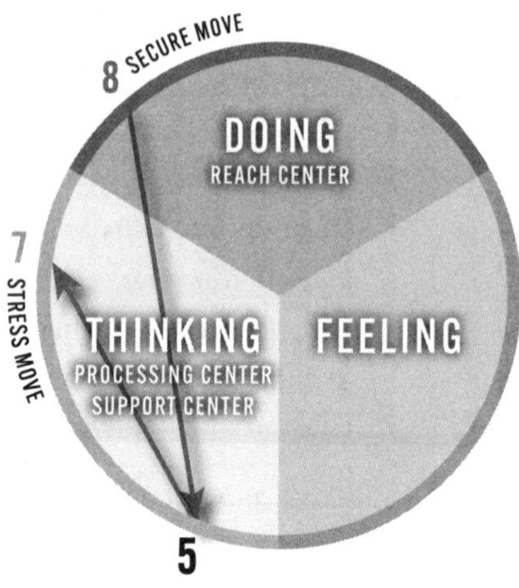

5s HOW FIVES VIEW THEMSELVES AT WORK	HOW OTHERS CAN VIEW FIVES AT WORK
I am a deep thinker.	You are aloof.
I value autonomy.	You are not a team player.
I am level-headed.	You are insensitive.
I am confident in my subject knowledge.	You are condescending.
I am thorough.	You don't consider others' timelines.
I enjoy theoretical discussion.	You are argumentative.
I have a limited social battery.	You are antisocial.

I LOVE FIVES. I'm not sure if everyone feels that way about the type at the end of their stress line, but I certainly do. It might have something to do with my family. Two of the most formative women in my life, my godmother and my maternal grandmother, are and were Fives. It might have something to do with my professional career. The best boss I ever had (see the chapter on Eights) is a Five. If we need the behaviors from our stress move to care for ourselves, it stands to reason that personal and working relationships with the type at the end of our stress line have the potential to be particularly nurturing. Ascribing to the view of the stress line as an ingrained support center equips me with a poignant visual of the Fives in my life who have all, in one way or another, uniquely and terrifically supported me.

My grandmother loved me with all of the practicality and emotional boundaries I craved as a child. My godmother has been one of my strongest advocates for nearly half a century—I could spend this entire chapter recounting the myriad ways she has supported me and not cover them all. My former boss is a true and dear friend. Then there is my father-in-law. I often wonder if, prior to his passing in 2019, he knew how grateful and aware I was of the subtle ways he chose to consistently land in my corner.

I am grateful for the HR manager in Baton Rouge. Our instant connection and effortless conversations about work and life remind me why I love what I do. I am grateful for the VP who moonlights as a young adult fiction writer. Her wisdom and pragmatic insight were invaluable as I started writing for publication. I am grateful for the Operations Manager in Alabama whose thoughtful responses to my social media musings on Fives are incredibly sustaining. I love Fives.

Being a Deep Thinker Versus Being Aloof

It is generally accepted that being in the Solitary Stance means that Fours, Fives, and Nines are difficult to read. Their internal terrain is a tapestry of private complexities that remain largely hidden from the outside world. As addressed in the chapters on Eights and Twos, there is a clear connection to what Fours, Fives, and Nines keep to themselves and their dominant center. As the thinking-dominant type in the Solitary Stance, Fives personify the Solitary Thinker. The thoughts of Fives are extremely private. If you want to know what a Five is thinking, you must ask questions that require more than a yes or no response. Even then, the Five will be notably measured with what thoughts they choose to share, and you will get a fraction of the totality of their mental collection.

This resonates deeply with me, as an Eight (line to Five). While my doing is independent and my feeling is responsive (line from Two), my thoughts are numerous, complex, and mine to hold. When you look at the Responsive Stance, Ones, Twos, and Sixes all share unfiltered thoughts by verbally processing and experience a higher degree of social comfort either as a precursor to processing out loud or as a result of it. Fives and Eights, by contrast, are likely the most socially awkward and definitely the most misunderstood types. This can be directly attributed to our solitary thinking.

Five's line to Seven means that they support solitary thinking with independent thinking. Independent thinking leads socially confident Sevens into most interactions with enthusiastic and unapologetic transparency of thought while keeping a treasure trove of ideas (line to Five) tucked away. This connection to Seven calls to mind a Five client who thoughtfully shared her ability to be the life of the party, noting that she has to make that choice ahead of time and build in plenty of time to recover after.

When Fives are comfortable shifting to the high side of independent thinking to share their experience of being the quintessential solitary or deep thinker, they offer helpful insight for the rest of us. Consider the reflection of a Five who is a VP for an insurance brokerage firm:

> As a Five, I am always thinking about a lot of things. Sometimes, it could be the very thing being discussed. Outwardly, it might seem like I'm daydreaming or am not present in the conversation, but I am. I'm just in my head about it, thinking through scenarios and wondering about at least fifteen things associated with the topic at hand.

Fives are the only type on the Enneagram for whom thinking supports thinking (line to Seven). With their last remaining intuitive option being a move to independent doing (line to Eight) and a strong likelihood of being surrounded by fellow employees who draw from thinking least or last, viewing Fives as aloof could be considered a foregone conclusion for those who work with them. Since solitary thinking is uniquely attributable to Fives, Sevens, and Eights and thus a foreign concept for many, it's helpful to consider the words of Thomas Edison: "The best thinking has been done in solitude."

Valuing Autonomy Versus Being a Team Player

Consider the words of a conscientious financial analyst and prison minister who, upon being promoted to Financial Operations Manager in his company, put a very Five spin on the open-door policy his new position warranted. His message for fellow employees: "My door is always closed . . . but you can open it." Such language is a refreshingly honest representation of the only type on the left of the processing divide who is not hardwired to cross over to the subjective or people-centric side.

The lines that Fives share with Seven and Eight keep them firmly planted on the left side of the divide, equipping them with the strongest natural desire for autonomy.

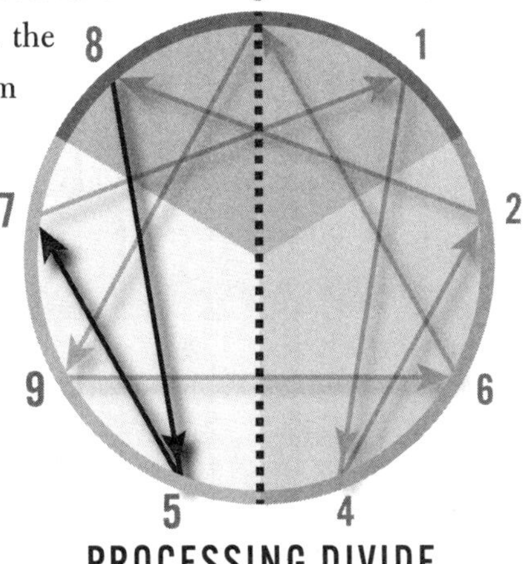

As established in the chapter on Threes, starting with a focus on others leads Twos, Sixes, and Nines to be categorically appreciated as team players. While Ones and Sevens join Fives in lacking an inherent ability to focus on or defer to others (no connection to Two, Six, or Nine), the One's fortified (support line to Four) position on the people-centric side of the processing divide and the Seven's move to cross the divide to engage doing (line to One) endow both types with a collaborative spirit. To be clear, it is not people that Fives inherently dislike, it is wasted or misused energy. Limited energy and capacity for a double task focus (line to Eight) equip Fives to prioritize autonomous work over teamwork as a general rule.

The hardwiring that keeps Fives from crossing the processing divide typically reveals itself in several ways. First and foremost, Fives do not enjoy meetings. When meetings shift off task, Fives are the first to notice. The verbal processing from Ones, Twos, and Sixes that accompanies a desire for affirmation and consensus is noticeably irksome to Fives who are not inclined to conceal their frustration with groupthink.

Fives and Nines tend to present very similarly at work. While a conversancy exists for the pairs who share a processing center and a stance, differing dominant center values color each type's reaction to lowered standards for doing (Eights versus Threes), feeling (Twos versus Sixes), and thinking (Fives versus Nines). Think of the connection between these pairs as blended family familiarity—they may share a house (processing center), but they come from different backgrounds (triads). While Nines shift to process with preferred thinking, they do not share the fast processing or impatience with illogical reasoning that is the hallmark of Fives.

Fives do not enjoy group projects. They discover this about themselves during their formative years in education and carry this realization into careers, often choosing paths that involve little to no collaborative tasks.

Fives do not enjoy blurring the lines between work life and personal life. The reigning theory when Covid-19 hit, forcing millions to work from home, was that Fives would be the biggest beneficiaries. In truth, Fives struggled greatly if working from home meant the loss of a clearly defined start and end to their workday.

Being Level-Headed Versus Being Insensitive

Despite being a feeling-dominant type and a thinking-dominant type, the notable similarities between Threes and Fives are intriguing. Both types have the innate ability to disconnect from emotion, a trait that contributes to their presentation of levelheadedness. Both generally carry an intuitive distaste for personality typing systems because neither type wants to be known intimately. The Enneagram pulls back the "Oz curtain" on Threes, which ultimately threatens their ability to succeed through image crafting. In the logical minds of Fives, the Enneagram categorizes human beings, something they see as fundamentally fallible.

A principal difference between Threes and Fives is the disconnect from anger. While Threes are masterful at disconnecting from any negative emotion, the singular emotion that Fives rarely disconnect from is anger. This failure to disconnect, combined with a natural dismissiveness, often leads Fives to mistype and be mistyped as Eights.

> Fives and Eights are the only two types on the Enneagram who show up to work without feeling or responsiveness. Everyone else brings one or both. Ones, Twos, and Sixes are responsive, Twos, Threes, and Fours are feeling dominant, Twos, Fours, and Sixes process with feeling and Sevens and Nines cross the processing divide early via their responsive lines to One and Six.

Their intuitive lack of feeling and responsiveness, combined with solitary thinking, contributes to the overwhelming perception of Fives and Eights as insensitive, and this hardwiring specifically exacerbates the broad cultural nonacceptance of female Fives and Eights. As an Eight, I am acutely aware of the injustice that accompanies making sweeping judgments about Fives and Eights without drawing from logic or objective reason. I am able to find compassion for those who judge us unfairly by accessing feeling and responsiveness through my connection to Two. Fives do not have that luxury.

As established, Fives and Sevens have no direct line to the Feeling Center. While both types are lightning-fast processors of information, their ability to process emotion is generally significantly delayed by contrast. Sevens are able to compensate for this delay through responsive doing (line to One). As we will explore in the following chapter, Sevens tend to fool themselves and others that they connected to emotion simply by being responsive. Fives are the only type on the Enneagram with no connection to the Responsive Stance (One, Two, Six). If Enneagram understanding equips us to do nothing else, let it be that we stop expecting from others what they don't intuitively have to give.

For every other type, responsiveness is innate. We are setting ourselves up for disappointment each and every time we require a response from

Fives on our terms. Rather than rebuking Fives for being insensitive or uncaring, working well with Fives might require taking note when Fives are responsive. For, unlike the rest of us who all have responsiveness hardwired in, when Fives respond, they made a conscious choice to do so.

Confidence Versus Condescension

Fives, by nature, are lifelong learners. Having a processing and support center in thinking and an ability to disconnect from emotion equips Fives to be the most objective and neutral type on the Enneagram. I have never met a Five who believed they knew everything there was to know about any given topic. Being a lifelong learner instills a certain level of humility regarding the vastness of knowledge and what one is able to glean from that in a lifetime. Fives spend their lifetimes as sponges, soaking up every detail they can find when a topic particularly interests them and absorbing more than most when a topic doesn't.

As noted previously, solitary thinking combined with a lack of feeling and responsiveness lead Fives and Eights to be the most socially awkward types. The social awkwardness of Eights is known intimately by the Eight but remains largely unseen by others. Their position in the Independent Stance equips Eights with high self-confidence and an independent reference point while their line from Two equips them with responsive feeling. Eights can walk into any situation and command the room while standing independent from the room. Their ability to draw from people awareness and responsiveness in Two keeps them connected enough to others to avoid the semblance of awkwardness.

By contrast, Fives have no direct connection to people awareness (Two, Three, Four) or responsiveness (One, Two, Six). What Fives do have is a double connection to the Independent Stance (lines to Seven and from Eight). The flip side of being the only type not equipped with responsiveness is being the only type doubly equipped with self-confidence and independence. When Fives are not enjoying the solitary comfort that an internal reference point provides them, their only option for engaging the world is through the confident assertiveness of independent thinking (Seven) or independent doing (Eight). Confidence in the absence of people awareness generally leads to others being more cognizant of the Five's social awkwardness than the Five.

Fives have the most social comfort when space is afforded for them to share their curated knowledge on any topic of interest. There is a delightful innocuous nature to their delivery of information when presenting to an interested audience. This reality is likely the driving force behind the beloved nature of Fives in academia. For the countless Fives who do not find themselves in the classroom or lecture hall, an uninterested or disengaged audience inevitably pushes them to draw from cynicism or sarcasm in their engagement of others. When a Five is regarded as condescending, innate cynicism as opposed to confidence has colored the Five's delivery.

While a cynical outlook can be experienced by any type on the Enneagram, deductive reasoning suggests that it would be instinctive for the type whose layered thinking in a largely feeling and doing-dominant world inhibits them from sharing a viewpoint with those around them. Fives are called "the observer" for a reason. Being a lifelong learner contributes to this reason, but the intrigue of those who see the world in starkly different ways leads discerning Fives to observe more than participate.

Being Thorough Versus Not Considering Others' Timelines

Not surprisingly, the consideration of others' timelines is consistently in question with Fives and Nines in the workplace. One would expect this to be an issue with all members of the Solitary Stance (Four, Five, Nine) where doing is engaged least or last. But the Four's position on the subjective action side of the processing divide and their double connection to responsiveness (lines to Two and from One) preclude them from being considered unresponsive. Fives and Nines, with all of their blended family familiarity, are left to jointly and consistently fail to meet the timeliness expectations of their coworkers.

A notable distinction between timeliness expectations and the actual due date is rarely observed. Fives and Nines don't miss deadlines any more than any other Enneagram type is prone to, yet they are scrutinized far more than any other type for having a propensity to do so. Both types see the big picture and are competent strategists. If they don't know how to do something, Fives and Nines figure it out on their own. They would rather do their own research than take up valuable time by asking questions. Both types value autonomy and have an intuitive stubborn response to outside pressure, leading both to desire latitude in their work environments.

Perhaps the real irony lies not in others' collective responses to the perceived lack of timeliness of Fives and Nines, but in their collectively distinct engagement of Fives as opposed to Nines in the workplace. Not only do Fives start out with a task focus that is unavailable to Nines, they have access to additional task focus through their connection to Eight, making Fives highly proficient regardless of the workload. Yet scrutiny of Fives is usually much less forgiving than that of Nines. Whether it is the Nine's ability to connect effortlessly with the rest of us, their calm deference, or their talent for harmonizing conflicting points of view, we are kinder when Nines fail to meet our expectations.

If high level task completion is the goal, give me a Five to work with every day. Fives are extremely thorough in their assessment and follow-through. As the most objectively neutral type, Fives don't get distracted by the office politics that derail other types. Fives are extremely fast processors who invariably absorb nonessential information that consistently proves to be valuable down the line.

We have a tendency to get lulled by the Nine's ability to focus on us. When Nines are deferring to us, engaging us with their responsive thinking (line to Six), we lose sight of the reality that their doing is solitary. We may approach them initially with our own frustrations about their lack of transparency surrounding task completion only to leave the conversation feeling better, but without the tangible evidence we were seeking in our approach. Fives may not be able to defer to us (no connection to Two, Six, or Nine), but their independent doing is refreshingly transparent, meaning we will always know where we stand with our requests of Fives.

Theorizing Versus Arguing

A motivating need to be against does not mean that Eights are prone to argue or debate for sport. This is actually one of the most common misconceptions about Eights. I remember being approached at an Enneagram event when I was in my early twenties. An individual approached me by chiding an acquaintance of his whom he had mistyped as an Eight. This man described his friend as an individual who sparked debate with others whenever they went out socially. Even if an Eight is a socially dominant subtype, our energy is not spent in the exchange of ideas and theory. Debate for sport is both too steeped in thinking and too relational for Eights. We have no need for others to see something from our point of view, especially if the others in question are strangers.

Fives, on the other hand, are contrarian by nature. They intuitively assuage social awkwardness through debate. It is often the only way they feel comfortable engaging others because it levels the playing field. Fives may not be equipped with the social graces that come easily for others, but that void is indistinguishable amid theoretical discussion. And very few individuals can rival the wealth of knowledge that Fives have neatly tucked away on any number of topics. It is helpful to remember that a Five who is engaging others, even if it is argumentative or awkward, is generally a better sign than one who isn't. If the Five is choosing to engage, it means they have not dismissed you.

The misconception of arguing as a definably Eight characteristic also regularly surfaces when applying an Enneagram lens to parenting. The majority of parents who mistype their child to tween as an Eight do so based on their child's penchant for argument. Eights either adhere to authority or stand independent from it—arguing simply doesn't factor in. Early and often, Five children deal with their own distaste for being told what to do by argumentatively pushing timelines and parameters.

Regardless of age, Fives want to be engaged with objective reason. As soon as you lead with emotion and a subjective lens, you lose with a Five.

I refer to a common characteristic of uniquely extroverted Fives as "poking the bear." This tendency largely defines the way that more socially comfortable Fives (who tend to mistype as Sevens) engage others at work. Whether it be boredom or curiosity, these Fives generally deal with both through social experimentation. Poking the bear can take many forms. It could be making a definitively polarizing comment and then stepping back to watch both sides hash it out. It could be making an off-color remark in a deceptively off the cuff manner before stepping back to watch the reactions fly. It could be targeting the high-strung rule followers by blatantly ignoring an established rule or procedure. Regardless of the method, these Fives can unwittingly cause real damage to team dynamics and productive workflow.

Having a Limited Social Battery Versus Being Antisocial

The non-negotiable for Fives is having a limited social battery. Think of a gas tank when visualizing the Five's finite store of energy. Regardless of the tank size (some Fives have a larger social battery than others), engagement with other people drains it.

This visual effectively sets the stage to discuss the anticipation that fuels Fives. Their social battery is intrinsically tied to the fear of losing autonomy, so Fives employ anticipation to ensure solitude when their battery is low. Whether Fives ever learn the Enneagram or not, they are acutely aware of their energy levels. Their anticipation is revealed to the rest of us through the three questions that Fives typically ask as they consider engagement with others in light of their social battery. Whether it be a meeting for work or a rendezvous that is more social in nature, Fives want to know: (1) What time does this engagement begin? (2) What time does this engagement end? and (3) Who is going to be there?

Fives take communicated beginning and end times seriously and are less likely to join if attendance is optional and times are fluid. Knowing who will be in meetings and social engagements is also key to their planning. People who are more emotional or talkative or lack personal boundaries drain Fives much faster than others. Don't let the Five's anticipatory questions deter you from including them. Fives want to be included. Established personal boundaries should not equate to being antisocial. Unfortunately, Fives are often considered misanthropic as a result of their calculated attempts to engage the rest of us on their terms.

There is a version of antisocial—objectionable, disruptive, rebellious—that tends to surface more with extroverted Fives and Nines with an Eight wing who mistype or are mistyped by others as Eights. While introversion and extroversion are not functions of Enneagram type and thus can be present regardless of type, there are very few extroverted Fives and Nines and even fewer introverted Eights.

The principal difference between extroverted Fives and Nines with an Eight wing who have mistyped as Eights and true-to-type Eights is antisocial behavior and a lack of intensity. Fours and Eights are intense. Other types may temporarily exhibit intense emotions or actions, but intensity is core to Fours and Eights alone, which contributes to the reality that Fours and Eights are the least likely to mistype themselves. While Eights are aggressively motivated, they are no more aggressively behaved than other types. Intensity, passion, and blunt transparency are not chosen behaviors to elicit a response from others. The conflict that energizes Eights surrounds actual injustice and righting wrongs on behalf of those who cannot do it for themselves. Combative behavior engaged for sport or to get the attention of another is a conscious choice available for other types not already motivated to be against.

Whether Five or Nine with an Eight wing, extroversion does not override an internal reference point or finite energy. Nines, who have the least energy on the Enneagram, admit to gleaning energy from others that they cannot sustain on their own. Extroversion enhances what low energy Nines with an Eight wing can draw from others if it is not transferred to combative behavior. Fives are aware that people are an energy drain, regardless. Extroversion simply equips them with a larger tank.

TIPS FOR MANAGING OTHERS, AS A FIVE

Your door cannot remain closed.

- If an open-door policy is unsustainable, set and keep regular "open-door" hours.
- Go to your employees to engage them. Walk to their desk or office. Take them to lunch. Join the office celebrations that are personal (birthdays, engagements, babies, etc.).
- You may not need to hear from your team with the frequency that they need to hear from you. If you think you are engaging too much, it is almost enough.

Nobody else shares your affinity for logic.

- While Sevens and Eights can meet you in logic, they need you to meet them in action. Threes share your ability to disconnect from emotion, but what you replace with objective reason, they replace with action. Remember that all three can match your processing speed.
- Ones, Twos, and Sixes likely make up a large percentage of your team and do not employ logic when making decisions at work. You will be able to satisfy both of your needs by working together to implement objectively sound systems and processes.
- Fours and Nines share your internal reference point and have high EQs. Lean on them to be competent guides for the people awareness and responsiveness you do not inherently possess.

Leading people will never give you the satisfaction that completing tasks provides.

- Moving into leadership is a nod to your contributions that will ironically make you feel like you are no longer contributing. That will never be true.
- Nobody appreciates autonomy at the level that you do. One of the best ways to engage your team is by sharing what you learned when you were in their shoes.

- You may not think meetings are necessary, but they are. It is okay to set up buffers to conserve inevitable energy depletion on meeting-heavy days.

TIPS FOR MANAGING A FIVE

Honor personal boundaries.

- Don't pull Fives into meetings unless their input is necessary. This not only benefits the Five, but the rest of the team.
- If you need a Five beyond the established work hours, let them know in advance and don't make it a habit without changing the terms of their employment.
- Don't put a Five on the spot in a meeting with others. If you want a Five's input (and you do), let them know when you schedule the meeting.

The task focus of Fives will benefit you greatly if you let it.

- Give Fives autonomy in all the ways that are reasonable.
- Lean on Fives for efficiency and sustainability checks. If something isn't working, the Five will let you know if you ask them.
- Fives have the ability to stand and deliver with relative ease when they are confident with the subject matter and there is no expectation of spontaneity. Don't ask someone else to present what is in the Five's purview unless the Five specifically requests it.

Be clear and objective with your expectations.

- Fives are misunderstood at work and do not have the energy nor the capacity to read social nuance.
- If team gatherings are mandatory, stick to that. Don't let the Five argue or "no show" their way out of it.
- Don't require responsiveness from Fives that they don't have to give. Avoid small talk and too many personal questions. Model that for everyone else on the team.

ENNEAGRAM SEVEN

Are we having fun yet?

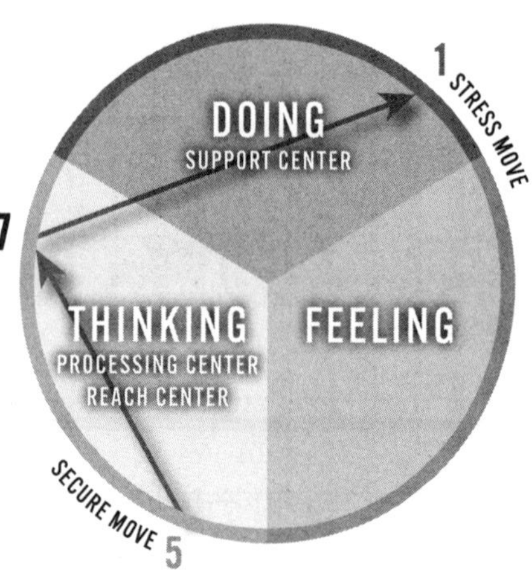

7s HOW SEVENS VIEW THEMSELVES AT WORK	HOW OTHERS CAN VIEW SEVENS AT WORK
I am optimistic.	You ignore the problem.
I quickly become interested in ideas.	You lack focus.
I enjoy engaging others.	You are cunning.
I don't take things too seriously.	You don't take anything seriously.
I love to brainstorm and plan.	You don't want to do the work.
I am a swift processor.	You get bored easily.
I know what I want.	You are self-centered.

IF YOU HAVE ARRIVED at this point by reading the chapters in order, you may have noticed that the tone of the chapters on Nines and Fives varies a bit in comparison to the chapters on the other Enneagram types. Maybe you found the tone less reproving or the call for balance less challenging. If that is the case, please consider this advance notice that this chapter will follow suit.

The shift in tone has little to do with my adjacent (Eight) position on the thinking side of the processing divide and much to do with the reality that, as the only thinking processors, Fives, Sevens, and Nines approach work and life with a distinctly "live and let live" attitude. Take that in for a moment while you consider your position on the processing divide. I consult a conscientious One Operations Manager who, in reference to admitted irritation with a Seven coworker, asked me recently if she was overthinking. I gently reminded her that objective reason wasn't fueling her irritation, "overfeeling" was. If you are losing sleep over your own vexations with thinking processors, rest assured, they have not noticed and are sleeping soundly.

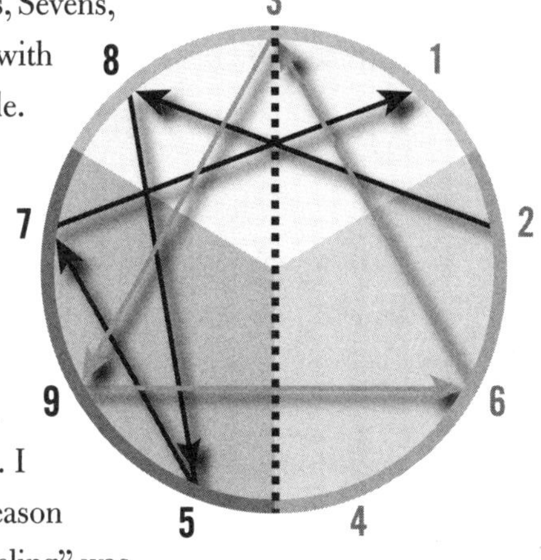

Being Optimistic Versus Ignoring the Problem

Adhering to the theme of non-negotiables, the box that has to be checked to be a Seven is living life in the positive half-range of emotion. Sevens join Threes and Eights in the Independent Stance with a glass-half-full mindset. While the optimistic arrival point is shared for these three types, their intuitive tactics for getting there are distinct. Eights replace negative emotion with anger. Because anger is fueling for them, they don't consider it negative—it is natural. Why be sad when you can be angry? Threes disconnect from negative emotion and project positivity in its place. Their poker face is unrivaled.

Because Threes and Eights have a direct connection to the Feeling Center, they achieve optimism through their manipulation of the emotion itself. Sevens don't have a line to the Feeling Center. Optimism for Sevens is therefore achieved not by adjusting the feeling but by adjusting the narrative. When a thinking-dominant Seven reframes, they are not reframing emotion, they are reframing their cognitive reception of what is happening. It is generally understood in personal and working relationships with Sevens that "the problem," more often than not, is getting the Seven to realize and acknowledge that there is a problem. Because Sevens reframe the situation to align with their positive view, they rarely see the problem as problematic.

Since the Feeling Center is also the human-centric Center of Intelligence, a people-awareness element is tied to the coping mechanism of Threes and Eights. If not for people, the Oz curtain would not be necessary for Threes. The projection of positivity is a Three's most innate form of image crafting—a means to achieve success in the eyes of others. Eights focus their anger and intensity on the problem, and if the problem is another person, the Eight will not hesitate to directly address that problem, in person.

The feeling void ingrained in the coping style of Sevens often leads them to be negligent in their capacity to address issues with coworkers. This reality typically surfaces in one of three ways. First is the "it's all good" stance. In this stance, Sevens stand independent from the problematic employee rather than respond to the issue by engaging them in any way. This out of sight, out of mind approach is the most common. Second is the tongue-in-cheek approach. A Seven will jovially acknowledge the unaddressed issue through satire and witty banter. This approach is most often taken in front of others. The third and final response usually indicates a move toward stress when the Seven sees people, in general, as the problem. In this space, Sevens are notably irritated by everyone. They will have a short fuse with the problematic employee and an even shorter fuse with the coworker who approached them to address the problem.

Quick Interest in Ideas Versus Lacking Focus

The inevitable reality for Sevens who are lightning-fast thinking processors fueled by anticipation is "monkey mind." The term "monkey mind" originates in Chinese folklore and describes the human state of restlessness and chaotic thoughts. In ancient Chinese legend, Sun Wukong, the Monkey King, is a rebellious trickster, inclined to mischief. Sound like any Sevens you know?

According to lore, Sun Wukong sets out on a journey to India in search of enlightenment and eventually becomes a faithful disciple of a Buddhist monk. His journey is regarded as a metaphor for the Buddhist path of spiritual development. The Buddhist term *kapicitta* or "monkey mind" describes the "agitated, easily distracted, and incessantly moving behavior of ordinary human consciousness." While neuroscience has supported the Buddhist understanding that all humans can experience monkey mind to varying degrees, it is the most natural state for Enneagram Sevens.

Anticipation amplifies the Seven's natural delight in unlimited possibilities. Their energy for action is fueled by the open-ended question: What's next? This is a terrific space to consider how shared fear and anticipation uniquely drive members of the Head Triad (Five, Six, Seven) in light of differing reference points and focuses. Fives fear loss of autonomy. They reconcile this fear internally by anticipating what others will require of them. Fives satisfy their need for autonomy by focusing on tasks. Sixes fear loss of control. They reconcile this fear externally by anticipating what could go wrong. Sixes satisfy their need for control by focusing on others. Sevens fear loss of freedom. They reconcile this fear independently by anticipating what's possible. Sevens satisfy their need for freedom by focusing on self.

The self-focus of Sevens ultimately determines whether they will be successful in overcoming a natural aversion to a single-pointed focus. While Sevens may struggle to maintain a single pointed focus, intuitive connection to task focus (lines to One and from Five) means that Sevens are more equipped than most to be able to focus on the task at hand. When a Seven is interested in the task or completing the task serves their personal agenda, their capacity for a double task focus clicks right into place and a Seven engages productive doing with alacrity. Alternatively, if the Seven is disinterested and the task does not serve a personal agenda, they will use the same task focus to derail themselves and others by prioritizing noncritical or unnecessary doing.

Acknowledging that intrinsic motivation does not change, effective tactics for motivating Sevens to focus at work ultimately come down to whether your expectations of the Seven align with their personal agenda. Remember, Sevens have no connection to Two, Six, or Nine and thus are ill-equipped to defer to the agendas of others. If your agenda aligns with the Seven's, everyone benefits from their positive energy and focus. If your agenda does not align, you would do well to find the "carrot" to dangle that motivates the Seven to align their agenda with yours. For a carrot to be successful, it must ultimately satisfy the Seven's desire for freedom to anticipate the possibilities of what's next.

Engaging Others Versus Being Cunning

Consider the dual realities that Sevens have no direct connection to people awareness in the Feeling Center and yet experience an extremely high degree of social comfort.

> Our son Sam, like all Sevens, has enjoyed a history of effortless social ease. Even as a toddler, we would leave whichever play place Sam had explored that day with a mini throng of children jubilantly chanting their goodbyes to him, by name. His formal education up to this point has included every possible parent notification for mildly disruptive behavior, from the drought of smiley faces on preschool behavior charts to high school detention. The inevitable follow-up meetings that placed my husband and me in front of teachers and administrators who gushed with their affection for Sam might have been confusing had we not known that our child is an Enneagram Seven.

Sevens are known for being exceedingly charming—better yet, disarming. They have genuinely good hearts, are inherently kind, and have a sincere affection for others. When they do bring levity (which is often), it is never at someone else's expense. They are always inclusive and do a masterful job of engaging individuals who are less socially adroit. Their confidence and general good nature open doors that remain closed for others. They have the unique gift of being able to engage the rest of us without needing anything in return. All of this works in the Seven's favor as they navigate the world.

Their innate ability to disarm allows Sevens to push boundaries without receiving consequences, and when they do want something, they generally get it with relative ease. I consult a hospital physician who reflected on a Seven who is newly in her charge. This Seven has never been written up and is generally known for things always going his way. A fellow physician was recently sharing with the Seven how much she enjoyed an infrequent trip to another floor for a popsicle on her break but always felt like the nurses on that floor disapproved of her making the trip, rare as it was. The Seven offered to bring this physician a popsicle any time she desired, recounting that he had enjoyed a popsicle one time, long ago, and now every time he is on that floor, those disapproving nurses offer him a popsicle as soon as he is in their vicinity.

When you consider all the ways that Sevens might go about getting their way so often, the only realistic options are above board. Sevens aren't conniving. They are transparent with their personal agendas. They don't skirt consequences by being deceptive, and yet, we don't want to alter their infectious positivity by doling out those consequences. Their inherent ability to stand independent from others while gaining so much from others begs the question, How does motivation void of the people-centric Feeling Center explain such a phenomenon?

One way to approach this question is to consider the striking similarities between Sevens and feeling processing Twos and Sixes when it comes to engaging others.

Consider two groups we have already analyzed—doing processors and the Solitary Stance. Eights, Ones, and Threes all process with the Doing Center. These "motors" personify action and implementation. Alternatively, the internally referenced members of the Solitary or Withdrawing Stance (Fours, Fives, Nines) engage the Doing Center least or last and can be viewed as the opposite of doing processors. If Eights, Ones, and Threes represent a green light or universal "go," Fours, Fives, and Nines represent a red light or universal "stop." As previously mentioned in the chapter on Fours, Solitary types personify the solitude and introspection that await all of us based on the lines that we share with those types.

When you consider the remaining three types, Twos, Sixes, and Sevens have a connection to doing in Eight (line from Two), Three (line from Six), and One (line from Seven). While these types do not process with doing (green light), their move to action is considerably faster than the types in the Solitary Stance (red light), making Twos, Sixes, and Sevens the yellow light or universal "yield." As the three types who engage doing second, these three personify social awareness and versatility. They intuitively lean into others' perspectives with curiosity. They recognize and acknowledge inherent strengths in others. And they recognize situational demands and opportunities. We all have a line connecting us to Two (Fours and Eights), Six (Threes and Nines), or Seven (Ones and Fives), so we all have the intuitive ability to engage social awareness and versatility and yield before doing.

Sevens are hardwired to draw from the Feeling Center least or last. While social awareness and versatility give the semblance of drawing from the people-centric Feeling Center (where Twos and Sixes process), Sevens are not able to authentically draw from feeling until they stop in the solitude and introspection that Five offers them. As the only yielding type without an ingrained ability to defer, the Seven's comfortable engagement of others can be misconstrued as calculatedly cunning.

Not Taking Things Too Seriously Versus Not Taking Anything Seriously

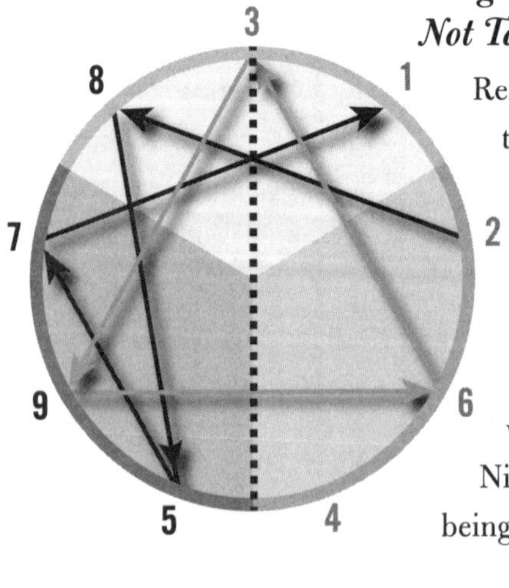

3
8
1
7
2
9
6
5
4

Remember that there are only four types who bring logic and objective reason to work without having to consciously reach for it. Fives, Sevens, and Nines process with the thinking that supports the doing processing of Eights. The withdrawing nature of Fives and Nines generally precludes them from being at the table where decisions are made, and if they have earned a seat, their internal reference point limits what they choose to offer. Self-confidence, swift processing, and assertiveness likely place Sevens and Eights at the table more often than Fives and Nines. However, feeling least or last does little to ingratiate them with the subjective right side of the divide.

When feeling is involved, all types can take ourselves too seriously. The beauty of being an optimistic reframer with no direct connection to feeling is that Sevens rarely, if ever, take themselves too seriously. This reality is a direct contributor to their natural charisma. The issue for Sevens, then, is not lack of self-awareness but lack of awareness of others. On point comedic timing fails considerably when situations call for sobriety.

The jokester feature of the Seven's personality is a key point where there is typically a clear delineation between male and female Sevens. Much like there is a deficit of analysis on counterphobic Sixes and Nines with an Eight wing, there is not much available insight that allows for the lack of slapstick delivery in female Sevens. Male Sevens are notoriously known for infusing painful or uncomfortable moments with humor. Female Sevens, on the other hand, are more equipped to bear the weight of poignant emotions without deflection. As a result, female Sevens can present much more like Threes or Nines.

While the Seven's ability to positively reframe is considerable, an inevitable problem with reframing the narrative arises when others are part of that narrative. Nobody else in the narrative is reframing what happened, and they certainly aren't looking to the Seven to reframe it for them. Everyone (including Sevens) wants to be taken seriously at some point. Some obviously want that more often than others, and when those people are in a position to resolve issues at work, they tend to feel pretty strongly about Sevens not being at the table.

When Sevens are asked, "What do you wish others you work with knew about you?" they invariably respond with an answer that involves wanting to be taken more seriously because coworkers do not recognize their intellectual and emotional depth. This is precisely where a predilection for standing independent hurts them. Sevens live lifetimes of getting what they want from others without making concessions for others. While they are terrifically equipped to be problem solvers, Sevens will continue to be overlooked if they insist on bringing levity when solemnity is required.

Brainstorming and Planning Versus Not Wanting to Do the Work

I have been working with the VP of a media company for years who struggled, early on, to identify himself as a Seven. His Eight wing was so strong that he saw himself more in Eight and even tested as an Eight. One of several discussions that led him to give Seven serious consideration centered around anticipation and thinking before doing. This VP loves whiteboard sessions. He lights up at the prospect of sitting in a room with blank whiteboards on the wall (there happens to be one of these rooms across from his office) and brainstorming for hours—something that would not be enjoyable for Eights who lead with action.

As two of only three types with a future orientation to time and the only two of those three to incorporate thinking, Sevens and Eights are uniquely equipped for strategic planning. Though they are equipped for it, Eights will never revel in it like Sevens do because strategy does little to satisfy their fueling determination. Fueling anticipation, on the other hand, is arguably something that effective strategic planning requires.

Sevens encounter two inevitable issues as a result of their affinity for brainstorming. First, jobs, like life, require more doing than thinking. As I mentioned in part one, we can get away with not drawing from the Feeling or Thinking Centers, but living requires doing. Second, the people who work with Sevens may appreciate their thinking, but Sevens, like all types in the workforce, are ultimately evaluated based on the benefit their doing brings.

> Fueling anticipation is so real for our son, Sam, that we have learned to help him channel it into being a productive doer. Our slogan for Sam is "Work hard, play

hard." If we take away his freedom to delight in future possibilities by placing too many parameters on him, he shuts down and we lose doubly. We lose his spark and his ability to focus on the task at hand. Sevens love challenges and loathe expectations. So we are clear and consistent with our broad expectations of him, most of which center around him being a strong student, since that is his primary job as a sophomore in high school. When thinking inevitably outweighs doing for Sam, we rein in the focus on what's next with a reminder that meeting our established expectations for doing (task focus) must come first. Work hard, play hard.

Sevens lose more ground with coworkers than they realize when they avoid the task at hand. We value the ways that they make work more enjoyable, but when we look up from doing and Sevens are nowhere to be seen, the negative feeling we are left with has much more staying power, in the long run, than all the positivity they bring.

Swift Processing Versus Easy Boredom

Given the swiftly advancing technology behind search engines, it is relatively easy to determine the universality of any topic that might be of interest. Information abounds on the characteristics of good and bad listeners, and a Seven's hardwiring does not land them on any page where effective listening habits are listed. Sevens are not alone in this. Processing speed correlates to listening capacity. The greater the speed, the less capacity one has to be an effective listener. This tracks when you consider the listening habits of the fastest processors on the Enneagram: Threes, Fives, Sevens, and Eights.

As established, the stance with the greatest representation in the general population is the Responsive Stance. Ones, Twos, and Sixes need to verbally process their thoughts. Add Nines with their proclivity for offering multiple angles of thought when they feel comfortable sharing relatable objectivity, and you get an overwhelming number of people who require effective listening to get their point across. Without active listeners, Ones, Twos, and Sixes will not get to productive thinking, and Nines will not get to productive doing.

While the yielding Seven's inherent gift of social awareness places a certain amount of onus on them to be a better listener for the vast majority of people in their circles who will benefit from it, Sevens and Fives have an added hurdle that fast processing Threes and Eights don't have. No line to the Feeling Center (Two, Three, Four) and no line to shift their focus to others (Two, Six, Nine) means that Sevens will have to make a conscious and concerted effort to develop those skills. Ironically, that development lies in their connection to Five.

With no line to the Feeling Center, a Seven's authentic connection to feeling is only possible when they ground their thinking and engage in solitude and introspection. Fives are pensive by nature. When Sevens draw from Five and put a damper on their naturally frenetic anticipation, slowing their swift processing and focusing their attention inward, their ability to engage in deliberate thought will inevitably lead them to reflect on their relationships with others. In this space, Sevens find themselves able to objectively consider hurts or slights they may have caused that have been overlooked or reframed.

Engaging in the honest self-reflection available to Sevens in their secure move to Five is the gateway not only to bringing up feeling, but to improved focus. Part of consciously becoming a better listener will require a focus on not finishing the thoughts and sentences of others. Allowing a slower processor to speak without interruption goes a long way in a working environment. Consider a delightful female Seven in her final third of life who reflected that when she focuses on becoming more grounded, she is able to recognize and embrace the reality that she puts her heart into everything, especially engaging others.

Knowing What I Want Versus Being Self-Centered

It is important for all types to be mindful of the value of quid pro quo as it relates to high-functioning personal and professional relationships. Sevens unintentionally lull the rest of us into joining a personal agenda through their generous inclusivity, affable nature, and infectious enthusiasm. A significant portion of a Seven's delightful anticipation is sharing that anticipation with the rest of us. Their energy is captivating and our desire to be included is never rebuffed. The more, the merrier when a Seven is making plans.

Sevens are generous in other ways. As gluttons for experience, Sevens hold material possessions much more loosely than most and tend to go through life with a "what's mine is yours" mentality. I have yet to meet a Seven who doesn't live fully into the "recognizing and acknowledging inherent strengths in others" aspect of social awareness. Their effortless ability to elevate the rest of us is remarkable. All of these charitable traits combine to deepen our collective disappointment when Sevens don't respond enthusiastically to our proposed agenda.

Granted, Ones, Fives, and Sevens all have an innate inability to defer to others (no line to Two, Six, or Nine). But few people spend a significant portion of their lives going along with the agendas of Ones or Fives. Coworkers and friends of Sevens often lean into the incongruous use of *breathtaking* when contemplating what it is like to be with a Seven who is attempting to be obliging. Just as we expect our understanding of the definition of *breathtaking* to be positive, so too we expect, after spending such significant time aligning with their agendas, that Sevens will bring their trademark enthusiasm to align with ours. In reality, their reluctant alignment is actually breathtaking. Their withdrawal of energy in those moments leaves others feeling as though the air has been sucked out of the room. From the Seven's independent reference point, they are putting in the effort to be present with us when they prefer to be elsewhere. They do not seem to realize how insufficient that feels to the rest of us.

The Seven's fear of loss of freedom leads them to be incredibly generous with everything but the two things others desire most: their time and their energy.

TIPS FOR MANAGING OTHERS, AS A SEVEN

Be mindful of ways to show others that you can be generous with your time and energy.

- Develop effective listening habits by practicing with the people who will benefit from it most: Ones, Twos, Fours, Sixes, and Nines.
- Practice servant leadership by taking on tasks that no one else wants . . . but don't make a show of it.
- Don't hold others hostage with your energy withdrawal. If your team is worried about making decisions that don't align with your agenda, they will never gain the independence that you want them to possess.

Don't let a collaborative mindset keep you from recognizing the reality of your differences.

- Threes and Eights share your confidence, fast processing, and future orientation to time . . . and they process with action. Lean on them when it's time to go.
- Ones, Twos, and Sixes have expectations surrounding your responsiveness, and their external reference point means they are watching you closely and keeping score. Be intentional about your follow-through where they are concerned.
- Fours, Fives, and Nines have the least energy and censor themselves before engaging. Your energetic lack of self-censorship can be off-putting. Tone it down with them.

You have to be serious if you want to be taken seriously.

- Be aware of your tendency to blow up meetings for your amusement or to satisfy boredom. This is the quickest way to lose favor with your middle managers.
- Do not put your comedic whims in writing. The levity you bring, while effective in the moment, can be devastating for you and others when taken out of context.

- Don't handle serious issues with public teasing. Learn to say hard things in private. Your humor in front of others should never be the first time an employee learns about an issue that involves them.

TIPS FOR MANAGING A SEVEN

Be consistent with

- expectations. Inconsistent expectations will lead to inconsistent effort from your Seven.
- follow-through. When you set an expectation, make sure the Seven learns that you will follow up to ensure that expectation has been met.
- consequences. If you set them, assign them. Making allowances is the worst thing you can do while leading a Seven.

Variety is the spice of life.

- Sevens need to change it up. The more varied the tasks, the better.
- In order to maintain a productive task focus, Sevens need breaks and an occasional change of scenery.
- Look for ways to break the monotony of doing. Everyone will benefit and Sevens will be renewed by anticipation.

The ultimate goal is agenda alignment.

- Sevens are disarming. Know your decision and compromise threshold in advance.
- Dangle the carrot. An inspired Seven is absolutely invaluable.
- Don't confuse camaraderie with loyalty. Loyalty for Sevens lies with their freedom, and they do not pretend otherwise.

ENNEAGRAM SIX

Yes, but . . . why?

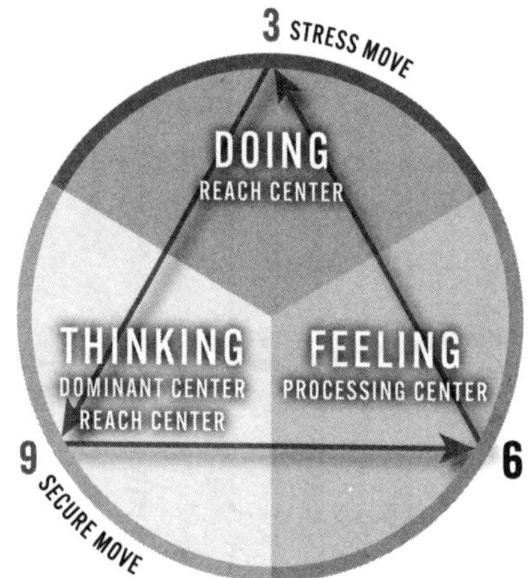

6s

HOW SIXES VIEW THEMSELVES AT WORK	HOW OTHERS CAN VIEW SIXES AT WORK
People are my priority.	You are too social.
I appreciate context and clarification.	You ask too many questions.
I want to trust authority.	You don't trust authority.
I see all sides.	You are contradictory.
I want to be sure.	You wait too long to make a decision.
I am loyal to people and processes.	You are resistant to change.
I've given this more thought than you.	You are controlling.

SIXES ARE PRESENTED in the final chapter for a reason. As you have read up to this point, the types who misidentify themselves most are Sixes, Threes, and Nines, in that order. It is no surprise that the primary types would be the most prone to mistyping. Being wired to shift away from your home base to process with a preferred center because you do not inherently trust your dominant center leads to very real imposter syndrome. If your filter, values, and fueling emotion are not linked to the center that you use to process, it makes sense that what follows would be an inability to believe that your success is tied to your intrinsic abilities. And you move through the centers faster than the six types whose stress and secure moves are not interconnected, leading you to see yourselves in every type.

Because Sixes doubt their own thinking, they generally talk themselves out of their initial reaction to being a Six before moving to mistype. Doubt, a disconnect from fear, and operating on a spectrum of phobic and counterphobic responses all contribute to the Six's propensity to mistype themselves. As mentioned in part one, while Sixes connect with inherent doubt, they often do not see themselves as fearful. Sixes repeatedly tell me that they are not afraid, but they are prepared for things to not go according to plan.

Of the primary types, only Sixes possess an external focus that absolutely tethers them to their environment. When a Six feels more secure in a given situation, they lean counterphobic and move toward action in Three to mobilize beyond natural doubt. Alternatively, when a Six feels less secure, they lean phobic and move toward research and reflection in Nine to wait until the environment changes or their feeling changes, whichever comes first.

Phobic versus counterphobic. When I consider all of my clients who are Sixes (and there are a lot), two of my all-time favorite work in different industries in the same state. The first could be the poster child for phobic Sixes. As the COO of a large holding company, he has taught me what it means to "feel impending doom" while mitigating risk at every turn. He is not too proud to admit that, while he is unquestionably loyal, he still goes to work every day fearing that he could be fired. And he is ready and willing to make the tedious intrastate drive between his companies as often as he needs because he can contemplate "hundreds of scenarios" that exacerbate his anxiety about flying on the company jet, and he has more control over the hundreds of scenarios that are possible on the ground.

The second is, without question, the most hardcore counterphobic Six I have ever met. As the bookkeeper for a network of radio stations, she gave me and the Enneagram the benefit of her doubt while I spent the better part of a year convincing her to consider Six for her core motivation and not Eight. She is fiercely loyal to her team, her boss, and her company. She has taught me that knowing how they are coming across rarely alters an aggressive delivery for Sixes. And she is a refreshing reminder that female Eights are not the only type who has to deal with the unfair expectations that surface from antiquated gender stereotypes.

I start this chapter with a nod to both because, while they lean heavily to the opposite ends of the Six spectrum of phobic and counterphobic responses, the COO has lived a lifetime that also encompasses counterphobic tendencies and the bookkeeper has had plenty of her own phobic moments. Much like the nondualism of the Enneagram, Sixes are not either phobic or counterphobic, they are both.

Prioritizing People Versus Being Too Social

Sixes have a motivating need to feel secure. A dominant Thinking Center provides them with an innate desire to gather as much information as possible to mitigate inevitable risk, but Sixes don't process with thinking, they process with feeling. Utilizing the people-centric Center of Intelligence to process means finding security in people, not information.

Feeling processors (Twos, Fours, and Sixes) need people. That makes sense. As members of the Heart Triad, Twos and Fours start with a relational lens, leading them to be more aware of what they are looking for in personal and professional relationships. An important distinction between Twos and Fours, who start with dominant feeling, and Sixes, who shift from the Thinking Center to process with feeling, is that an individual person can meet a Two's need to be needed and a Four's need to be understood. Sixes need more than a person to feel secure, they need people.

This reality can be observed in most professional environments. Once Twos and Fours establish a connection with the person who meets their motivating need, they are less inclined to spend an inordinate amount of time socializing. Twos shift from a focus on others to a task focus (line to Eight) and incorporate socializing while they are doing. Fours tend to alternate from a focus on others (line to Two) to a task focus (line from One) depending on which focus aligns with their position on the pendulum of internal fluctuations (core self-focus) at the time.

With no inherent task focus (no line to One, Five, or Eight), Sixes are the most prone to socialize at work. The valuable upside to this is community building. Sixes love to bring people together around a common theme or interest. They do not view their job description independent of people and thus do not view socializing as anything but an integral part of their function at work. Add their propensity to verbally process and you get a lot of talking. So much talking. Based on the reality that there are more Sixes and Nines than any other type, it can be reasoned that for all the Fives and Eights who don't have time for chit-chat, you'll find two to three times as many Sixes who want nothing else. Even the hardcore counterphobic bookkeeper admits to "loving chit-chat."

When you value information and socializing is your process, oversharing is inevitable.

Sixes connect with others through the sharing of personal information. They feel close to the people who matter to them when they know the details of what's happening in their lives on a regular basis. When a Six asks you how you are doing, they want as much detail as you are willing to provide, and they offer plenty in return (superfluous context). Sixes don't delineate between personal and professional relationships when it comes to exchanging information, which can sometimes catch coworkers off guard.

Sixes are known as the loyalist, the devil's advocate, and the true team player. Prioritizing people through a shift to process with feeling brings "true team player" to the foreground. Because community meets a Six's need to feel secure, they are strong advocates for their teams and do not make decisions without ample consideration for individuals and the team as a whole.

Appreciating Context and Clarification Versus Asking Too Many Questions

If a job can generally be summarized as doing that accomplishes objectives in a professional environment, while every type is universally equipped for this type of doing, Sixes and Nines are the only two types who engage ample prerequisite thinking and feeling before this doing can be realized. In addition to abandoning dominant doing to process with thinking, Nines struggle to believe that their presence matters. While doubling down on thinking equips them with plenty of objective reasons to delay action, it is not until they engage feeling and contemplate their real connection to people who are counting on them that Nines gain motivation to move forward with a task.

Sixes carry all of their dominant thinking values—information, data, analysis—with them to process with feeling. Thus, Sixes feel strongly about the integrity and free flow of information. Sixes are the only type who consistently need to know the *why* before they can move forward with a task. Without Enneagram familiarity, the invariable delay that exists for Sixes between receiving information and deciding to act can be confusing, if not frustrating. The Enneagram reveals the imperative stop that Sixes make to process information with feeling and their uniquely subjective view of the task in question.

Information gathering is a key initial step for all Sixes. As verbal processors with an external reference point who gain security from people, information gathering will include asking a lot of questions. Regardless of the environment, Sixes ask the most questions in their quest to feel secure. Consider the reflection of a terrific One Senior Executive VP who represents the necessary motor on a leadership team that is working to right the ship for a company I consult. He shared recently that he knows he can move forward in his current working environment when the Sixes at the table are on board. When we manage Sixes, it is a natural reaction to receive their barrage of questions as a calculated effort to question our leadership. That is very rarely the case with Sixes, who are one of the types least inclined to want to occupy the chair that makes final decisions.

Remembering what each stance needs from a professional environment to be successful is crucial for managing all types and can be particularly advantageous for Sixes who value information and analysis while needing people to ultimately make them feel secure.

The Independent Stance (Three, Seven, Eight) needs consistency to be most effective at work. Consistent authority, boundaries, and expectations must be present for independent types to give their best. Drawing from feeling least or last and abundant energy for action means that these types don't hesitate to make decisions with swift processing and self-confidence. A lack of consistency opens the door for Threes, Sevens, and Eights to broaden the illusion of control and operate independent from leadership, the team, or both.

The Solitary Stance (Four, Five, Nine) needs latitude in order to be most effective. Because outside pressure to do is met with intuitive stubbornness from these Solitary types who draw from doing least or last, exorbitant or unreasonable pressure will generally produce the opposite of a desired effect. Mutually agreed upon timelines that are arrived at by asking for input from the Four, Five, or Nine and that are honored without multiple check-ins create an environment where the Solitary Stance can be engaged and productive.

The Responsive Stance (One, Two, Six) needs affirmation at work, and this involves more than the obligatory pat on the back. Drawing from thinking least or last means that the Responsive Stance is operating with predominant feeling and doing. These types feel a strong desire to do well but are unable to objectively evaluate their work. Providing time and space for Responsive types to talk through their thinking while actively listening and offering feedback is paramount to setting up Ones, Twos, and Sixes for success.

Wanting to Trust Authority Versus Not Trusting Authority

Response to authority is perhaps the clearest space to identify phobic versus counterphobic leans with Sixes. Phobic-leaning Sixes start with trust until they are given reason to doubt, and counterphobic-leaning Sixes start with doubt until trust is earned. While the approaches are distinct, the motivation is the same. All Sixes, regardless of their lean, engage their external reference point and inherent focus on others to watch authority. Authority, in the mind of a Six, can be an individual, a team, a company, or an institution.

This is also the clearest space to distinguish between true Eights and Sixes who have mistyped as Eights. Whether Eights adhere to authority or stand independent from it, their focus is never on authority. Oppositional defiance is erroneously and much too often connected to young Eights. A negative reaction to authority requires a focus on authority that Eights do not have.

Although phobic-leaning Sixes start with trust, they can lead authority to believe that trust has not been earned when they spend so much time asking for clarification. All too often, we think that a Six's persistent questions indicate a lack of trust in us when, in reality, their intuitive responsiveness seeks to elicit feedback from us so they may feel confident moving forward.

A distinct pattern emerges with Sixes that centers around them asking rational questions while not seeming satisfied with rational answers. What we are missing when we allow ourselves to overinvest in this varied yet predictable rigmarole is the reality that Sixes process with feeling. Just as independent types share the tagline "It's not personal, it's business," we must remember when we engage with Sixes "It's not personal, it's Sixness."

Earning the role of trusted advisor with a Six does not mean that the Six trusts you enough to do what you suggest, it simply means the Six trusts you enough to ask for your suggestion. Six advisors would do well not to tether themselves to the outcome of a Six's subjective reasoning.

We cannot predict what will influence a Six to feel secure any more than the Six can.

Nowhere is this unpredictability more evident than the remarkably high correlation between phobic-leaning Sixes and a propensity toward cult thinking. My artist friend, Elizabeth, whom I introduced in the chapter on Fours, hosts the Austin Enneagram podcast, and in 2023, she interviewed a Six who shared her experience watching the NXIVM cult documentary with her husband. While they were watching, her husband asked aloud, "What kind of person could possibly get involved in something like this?" The Six's immediate answer was "Me." I recently shared this exchange with a delightfully self-reflective Six I am newly consulting, and she told me that she listens to podcasts on avoiding cults and cult thinking because she knows how prone she is to it.

Seeing All Sides Versus Being Contradictory

When I am working with Sixes who are new to the Enneagram and unsure of their type, they all give consistently similar cues. The first happens during our introduction. I like to start one-on-one sessions by asking my clients how they arrived at their particular position in that particular company. I intentionally leave the question open-ended by adding "include whatever you want to include." The time it takes Sixes to answer that question stands in stark contrast to every other type. Sixes invariably take more time and share a lot of personal details (superfluous context). When they finish, I know where they were born, where they went to school, their children's names and ages, etc.

The second cue usually happens while I am teaching the basics of an Enneagram introduction. Knowing that my intro is content heavy, I have built in natural breaks so my clients can process and ask questions. Sixes inevitably have questions before I get to the first break. The third cue happens every time, even if the first and second cues do not. When I ask Sixes situational questions, every answer is preceded by the Six's version of "it depends."

In the chapter on Ones, we analyzed Ones as responsive doers. As the doing-dominant member of the Responsive Stance, a One's doing is transparent and can be influenced. As the thinking-dominant member of the Responsive Stance, Sixes personify responsive thinkers. A Six's thinking is transparent and can be influenced. With enough information, you can change a Six's mind. While Nines are known for seeing both sides in conflict or disagreement, Sixes cannot help but see multiple angles all the time. This is precisely where they earn the moniker "devil's advocate." The contradictory thinking that is part of the hard-wiring of Sixes can make exchanges at work lengthy and frustrating.

As the only interconnected types, Threes, Sixes, and Nines ultimately think, feel, and do in similar fashion. Distinct fueling emotions, reference points, and orientations to time contribute to the ways they show up uniquely to engage the rest of us. In truth, the external reference point and verbal processing of Sixes end up coloring our judgment of them much more than Threes or Nines. While all three types represent responsive thinking, Sixes lead with it by engaging the rest of us when they are thinking out loud. Threes and Nines are responsive thinkers who don't verbally process, so they rarely pull us in to share thinking.

Sixes follow responsive thinking with independent feeling (line to Three). As the feeling-dominant member in the Independent Stance, a Three's feeling is transparent but cannot be influenced. We often misread the emotional transparency of Sixes as an open invitation to influence their feeling only to find that, while we can change their mind, we cannot change how they feel about anything. This trait is also observed in Threes and Nines.

Sixes seek us out and bring us into their world when they are trying to decide what action to take. Once engaged, we offer our input and then we wait . . . and wait, while the Six processes with independent feeling. We end up waiting much longer than we ever expected to find out what the Six ultimately decided to do because, like Threes and Nines, Sixes are solitary doers. As the doing-dominant member of the Solitary Stance, a Nine's doing is neither transparent nor influenceable. It does not occur to Threes, Sixes, or Nines to share their plan of action with the rest of us, leading to an inevitable anticlimax for those of us who were sought out by the Six when they were trying to decide what to do.

Wanting to Be Sure Versus Waiting Too Long to Decide

I consult a counterphobic-leaning Six who is the VP of operations at a company that manufactures organic flavors and fragrances and a phobic-leaning Six who built a digital marketing agency from the ground up. When presented with the question "What does it mean to be a Six?" these insightful gentlemen both provided answers that highlight the Six's desire for certainty tethered to a people-centric processing center and an external reference point.

Counterphobic Six, vice president of operations:

> If you were to ask me how I feel about myself and my decision-making, I would say I am very indecisive and lack confidence in what I do. That statement would be false and true at the same time. In truth, I am very decisive, almost bullish, when it comes to tasks or situations that I have already done or have a clear understanding of how it will affect others. The key word being *others* as most, if not all, of my decisions are based on how it will affect others and are not for my personal gain. My understanding of how actions will affect your surroundings or how actions will affect others coincides with my need for social interaction. Small group interaction, good or bad, is my tool to process quickly. Years of noticing how different individuals react to certain questions, tones, or statements allow me to go from indecisive to decisive and from unconfident to confident.

Phobic Six, president and founder:

> The biggest thing I identify with as a Six would be the decision-making process. I tend to think through the various options guided by my gut initially. Then, I like to discuss with a trusted advisor. This could include a mentor, business coach, or a friend that owns a similar business. I typically will also discuss with a key person or two that the decision directly affects. I usually want to get that person's buy-in or, at a minimum, give them a heads up that this decision is being considered. Sometimes I'll get conflicting perspectives from the people I solicit information from.
>
> This situation can sometimes be off-putting or confusing for those involved. For instance, I may discuss the situation with one

key employee that the decision affects, and I'll come out of that discussion agreeing with that employee. To the employee it may feel like we're on the same page. Then, I'll go discuss the same issue with another employee, and then I'll realize I agree with that employee's conflicting view. Coming away from that discussion the second employee believes we're on the same page.

The other piece is that this situation slows the entire decision-making process down. To me it's important to get buy-in from those involved, and to give them some time to understand the change that is about to happen. However, to other stakeholders such as our parent company or board of directors, it just appears to be a slow-moving decision-making process. I think stakeholders can easily also assume that I just sway from option to option without actually having a backbone to decide something. I think there could be a very small bit of truth to it, but to me it's just part of the evaluation process.

Loyalty Versus Resistance to Change

Sixes do not move forward, with speed, into unknown territory. Ever.

Consider, for illustrative purposes, a phobic Six and a counter-phobic Six standing at the base of a mountain they have decided to climb. Both Sixes look up at the mountain and are hit by the gravity of their impending decision. Both Sixes consider the likelihood of injury or death while climbing the mountain. Both Sixes turn to the Sherpa who will guide them on their journey up the mountain and begin their rapid-fire questions: Is there any chance we will not survive this climb? How many people have you successfully ushered up and down this mountain? Can I speak to any of those people? How does my age, ability, etc. compare to others who have made this climb? How sure are you that this climb will be successful?

When you consider the delineation between phobic leans and counter-phobic leans, it is helpful to remember that the motivating need to feel secure is the same for all Sixes. Their questions are the same because their hardwiring is the same. It is what they choose to do with the information they receive that causes Sixes to lean one way or the other.

The Six who leans phobic will take all of the Sherpa's answers and go home until their feeling changes or something in their external environment causes their feeling to change. The Six who leans counterphobic will take the Sherpa's answers and climb the mountain or "do it scared," a typical mantra for Sixes. The principal difference between a phobic and counterphobic lean for Sixes is the rate at which they choose to mobilize beyond their doubt.

All Sixes are resistant to change because all Sixes want a predictability that life rarely offers. Sixes search for patterns and consistencies everywhere in an effort to combat the inconsistencies that their minds inevitably create. When it comes to changes in leadership, phobic Sixes trust first and look to elevate the new authority. Counterphobic Sixes doubt first and carefully watch to make sure authoritative power is not misused.

Giving Something More Thought Versus Being Controlling

The depth of subjective nuance that characterizes a Six's processing is astonishing.

I was enjoying lunch one day with the counterphobic Six HR Director of a company that I consult. This company galvanizes steel, boasting the use of special high-grade zinc and the largest lead-free kettle in the South. Picture very large pieces of steel being lowered by crane into a massive kettle of molten zinc that is as long as a bowling lane and three times as wide. While we were at lunch, the Six received two calls within minutes of each other. One was from the head of the galvanizing plant and the other was from the head of the legal department. She did not answer either call, and both voicemails were nondescript.

We cut our lunch short, and by the time we paid our bill and reached the car, the Six had determined that an employee had fallen into the kettle. Before returning either call (which happened within fifteen minutes), she had already planned the details of a funeral down to the best catering option on short notice. When she returned both calls, she learned that there had been a minor glitch regarding the distribution of new insurance cards.

Sixes are, by nature, the most controlling type because Sixes know what it means to consider every angle and are acutely aware that the rest of us do not. I used to teach that Sixes were ruled by what-ifs. The more I work with Sixes, the more I realize how inadequate that generalization is. The layered thinking of Sixes is not based on a series of questions, but a series of solutions. Sixes don't theorize scenarios to justify fear, they theorize scenarios to overcome fear. And Sixes always have a plan.

Phobic Sixes tend to reconcile their desire for control through passive-aggressive behavior, much of which is channeled through verbal processing. Counterphobic Sixes tend to reconcile their desire for control through aggressive and domineering behavior. Either way, Sixes intuitively view themselves as loyal and fitting advocates for the rest of us because, while we may dismiss them as being ruled by what-ifs, they accurately see themselves as being secured by if-thens.

TIPS FOR MANAGING OTHERS, AS A SIX

Your verbal processing will not always be well received.

- Your comfort with the exchange of personal information can make others uncomfortable and can be viewed as unprofessional.
- Your own need to know why doesn't translate well. When assigning tasks, keep the details high level.
- Read social cues when engaging other employees and limit the time you spend in chit-chat. The last thing you want is to be avoided.

Your desire for control is real. So is everyone else's.

- Threes, Sevens, and Eights will stand independent from your overcontrol. Processing with the feeling that they use least or last means that you will lose in a standoff.
- Ones, Twos, and other Sixes have the same desire for control and the same external reference point. Avoid getting into the habit of watching them watching you.
- Fours, Fives, and Nines will not respond favorably to overcontrol, and you won't know it until it's too late.

You cannot change your responsive thinking. You can change your patterns.

- If you want the input of multiple employees, get them in a room together to avoid inevitable triangulation.
- Don't commit to an idea if you know you are going to seek additional input.
- Circle back to whomever you sought input from once you make your final decision.

TIPS FOR MANAGING A SIX

Questions are central to a Six's processing.

- Do not take their line of questioning personally. It's not personal, it's Sixness.
- Sixes can control time with questions. You will have to put boundaries on that time.
- Challenge yourself to mitigate the volume of questions by anticipating them and answering them in advance.

Create time and space to listen to Sixes. You want them on board.

- Sixes consider more angles than you ever will. The sooner you see that as a strength, the sooner you can figure out how to use that thinking to your advantage.
- Don't put Sixes on the spot. Publish meeting agendas ahead of time.
- When Sixes want to meet, ask for a summary of what they wish to discuss in advance. They need to verbally process with someone else before they get to you.

Find ways to offer affirmation.

- Sixes do well with a free flow of information.
- Practice active listening and offer feedback. The more feedback you give, the less they'll eventually need.
- Acknowledge the ways the Six individually contributes to the greater good.

PART II SUMMARY AND MISTYPING

Individual commitment to a group effort—that is what makes a team work, a company work, a society work, a civilization work.

Vince Lombardi

AS ESTABLISHED IN THE INTRODUCTION, the Enneagram can be a compelling tool for genuine collaboration in any environment because it fosters authentic self-examination, first. The ultimate effectiveness that extends from applying this lens to others is largely dependent upon the clarity with which we see ourselves.

While the Enneagram presents us with a natural order for viewing the Centers of Intelligence based on each center's contribution to observable behavior (doing, feeling, thinking), the unbiased objectivity that flows from thinking, when prioritized, maximizes the benefits of this universal wisdom. Consider an initially skeptical Five who shared his esteem for the Enneagram by calling it a "cheat code" for getting along with others. While his terminology may not align with my gut-centered desire for integrity, I appreciate the tangible practicality of his illustration and the trickle-down visual it provides. If we are able to equip ourselves to objectively distinguish between the Centers of Intelligence that inform nine distinct motivations (thinking), our sensitivity for others markedly improves (feeling), thereby enhancing our actions (doing).

The Reality of Mistyping

An estimated one-third of people mistype themselves when learning the Enneagram. Online tests for discovering Enneagram type consistently prove to be incorrect. This is not surprising when you consider the reality that the only unvarying dynamic in the use of written indicators is the presence of variables. Not only do the questions themselves vary greatly based on test and author, there are numerous factors that affect our answers: taking too long to think about answers, answering during stressful periods, answering based on false or hopeful perceptions of self, leaning into others' views of us—not to mention the propensity of indicators to gather data grounded in behavior rather than motivation.

Aside from the inevitable fallibility of online tests, we can all be prone to a subjective interpretation of information that creates natural blinders to acknowledging core motivation. One of the principal reasons a focus on non-negotiables for individual types is important is to combat a very real human tendency to avoid claiming our true type by focusing on indicative characteristics that do not apply while overinflating characteristics from another type that do apply. All of this is easier to do without a firm grasp on what each of the intelligence centers represents as they contribute to the way we uniquely see the world. Since typing correctly is crucial to realizing the effectiveness of this wisdom, let's close with a few practical tips for landing correctly on type. This can be achieved through an honestly self-reflective response to the following three questions.

1. How do I behave when I am stressed? Regardless of type, we are decidedly more cognizant of our stress thresholds than we are of the comfortable vulnerability that awaits us in balanced security. It is common, when learning the Enneagram in the context of a professional environment, to misidentify as a doing processor or motor (Eight, One, Three), because we are all engaging the Doing Center at work. Since there are only two types who withdraw and become more passive in stress, identifying your own stress response is a key step to avoiding mistyping. Eights (stress line to Five) and Threes (stress line to Nine) are the two types whose stress move draws them internally into objective thinking. If stress makes you bigger, louder, or more—more assertive, more emotional, more anxious, more intense—you are likely *not* an Eight or Three.

2. Am I conscious of my anger when it surfaces? My uneasiness within? My fear? Fueling emotions are so ingrained in our psyches, we are usually the least conscious of that emotion when it surfaces. Others will observe it in us long before we see it in ourselves, and we will be more accepting and understanding of the expression of that emotion in others.

Anger fuels Eights, Nines, and Ones. If you are conscious of your own anger when it surfaces, you are likely *not* an Eight, Nine, or One. If you are more sensitive to the expression of anger in others, you are likely *not* an Eight, Nine, or One.

Uneasiness within fuels Twos, Threes, and Fours. If it is easier for you to identify for yourself and share with others when you are feeling internal turmoil, you are likely *not* a Two, Three, or Four. If the expression of feelings from others makes you uncomfortable, you are likely *not* a Two, Three, or Four.

Fear fuels Fives, Sixes, and Sevens. If you are conscious of and feel compelled to share your fears with others, you are likely *not* a Five, Six, or Seven. If the expression of fear in others brings you discomfort, you are likely *not* a Five, Six, or Seven.

3. How do I react when the "world is blowing up" next to me? Our reference point tethers us internally, externally, or independently and does not change. Reference points have tremendous influence on the decisions we make. The most accurate way to identify your reference point is to consider your response to your environment.

Threes, Sevens, and Eights have an *independent* reference point. Their response to the environment is to stand independent. They can choose to act in response to what is outside of them, but that is a choice. Their motivation is to stand independent and be unaffected. If you have a tendency to withdraw from your environment or you are consistently motivated to respond to what is outside of you, you are likely *not* a Three, Seven, or Eight.

Fours, Fives, and Nines have an *internal* reference point. Their response to the environment is to withdraw mentally and/or physically. These types are most comfortable stepping back and observing their environment and are typically the last to respond, especially if there is outside pressure to act. If you feel a strong need to affect your environment or have more confidence being big in the room, you are likely *not* a Four, Five, or Nine.

Ones, Twos, and Sixes have an *external* reference point. They are tethered to their environment and are consistently motivated to respond to what is happening. These types feel strongly about collective awareness and responsibility. If your first instinct is to withdraw from your environment or you are able to affect the environment without being affected by it, you are likely *not* a One, Two, or Six.

CONCLUSION

WE DON'T INTENTIONALLY SET OUT to make life more difficult for ourselves or others. At work, as in all areas of life, disconnects and perceived slights are inevitable but do not have staying power when we embrace the reality that as human beings, we approach every situation from nine distinct ways of seeing. Not only does Enneagram understanding provide an insightful lens through which we can view ourselves and others with understanding and compassion, it equips us with a practical tool that wields the power to significantly improve our individual and collective engagement of thinking, feeling, and doing. There is a reason that bringing these centers into balance has been the focus of philosophers and theologians for centuries. Whether you utilize the Enneagram for personal, professional, or spiritual development, the benefits will be tangible and manifold—for you and for those with whom you spend your days.

ACKNOWLEDGMENTS

WITH GRATITUDE FOR MY GODMOTHER, Carolyn Teel. Regardless of the endeavor, you have been a pillar of support and encouragement since my birth.

With gratitude for my friend Tara Mills. You have shared with me the most precious and unexpected gift of being the enthusiastic Eight in my corner.

With gratitude for my clients Kenny Robison and Flynn Foster. Your humble trust in the effectiveness of this tool gave me the necessary runway to develop Enneagram language for cohesive teamwork in every industry.

With gratitude for the following conscientious stewards of the Enneagram. You have uniquely broadened the scope of this wisdom without exploiting it for commercial gain.

- Elizabeth Chapin, *Austin Enneagram*: You foster meaningful conversation with your guests that never ceases to produce authentically fresh insight.
- Jeff Cook and TJ Wilson, *Around the Circle*: You so graciously give new voices and new ideas (including my own) a platform.
- Russ Hudson, *The Enneagram Institute*: You embody the wisdom that flows from achieving balance between feeling and thinking.
- Courtney Perry, Yenneagram: Your exploration of the intersection of Enneagram and somatic practices is exciting and important.

- Richard Rohr, Center for Action and Contemplation: You paved the way for the rest of us to take the Enneagram off the page and put it into meaningful practice.
- Suzanne Stabile, *The Enneagram Journey*: You pioneered making the Enneagram universally relatable by teaching through storytelling.
- Brittany Thomas, Enneagram Explained: You promote the practicality of this wisdom in a way that is relevant and accessible.

Appendix A

WINGS

FOR THOSE WHO ARE NEW to Enneagram understanding, wings may be a factor in determining their number. Enneagram wings are simply the numbers on either side of our core type.

Wing acknowledgment is in an appendix for a reason. Once Enneagram type is known, wings matter very little because they have no influence on core motivation and do not interfere with nor assist with achieving balance among the Centers of Intelligence.

It is generally understood that our behaviors can be influenced by one wing in the first half of life, and we intuitively allow influence from the other wing in the second half. It is just as possible to have wings that do not affect behavior as it is to have a strong wing. Wing strength ultimately refers to the level of influence that number has on our behavior. I am what I refer to as a "straight up Eight," which means that I do not have a strong Seven or Nine wing. I can identify the mild influence of my Seven wing in my childhood and early adulthood, amplifying Eight behaviors with additional independent yet more playful energy. I also recognize the budding influence of my Nine wing in my forties. Working to be more balanced and react less intensely to the world in my efforts to be more approachable opens an instinctive connection to Nine.

Having a strong wing can affect the time it takes to land on core type. Eights are the only gut-centered independent type. When Eights hear about the Enneagram, we settle on our type quickly and without reservation regardless of wing influence. For individuals struggling to land on type, Eight should not be an option. Eights don't manufacture self-assuredness. It just is. A strong Eight wing has notable influence on Sevens and Nines alike and may lead Sevens and Nines to mistype as Eights.

After Sixes, who consistently have the most difficulty landing confidently on their type, the next space where initially identifying core number may present a struggle is for Nines with a strong One wing and Ones with a strong Nine wing. Sometimes, the meticulousness inherent to Ones affects the way higher functioning, more productive Nines hear themselves in Enneagram descriptions. Alternatively, the introspectiveness of core Nine may skew the ways introverted Ones take in Enneagram knowledge to discover their type.

In two spaces, wings can dramatically skew the way a specific type presents in comparison to their core type counterparts. These spaces are created by contradictory motivations and Centers of Intelligence.

First, the two wings that represent opposing motivations: a Nine with a strong Eight wing and a Three with a strong Four wing. (This does not apply in reverse. A Nine wing does not skew Eight presentation, and a Three wing does not skew Four presentation.) Most Nines intuitively lean toward a One wing. Nines with an Eight wing present very differently from other Nines. Nines with an Eight wing are dealing with dueling impulses: the Nine desire to avoid conflict versus the Eight desire to engage in it, and the Nine lack of energy versus the Eight abundance of it. Nines with Eight wings are noticeably feistier and more outspoken than other Nines. The Eight wing influences these Nines to "write checks" that they aren't hardwired to cash. They will jump into conflict with the speed and assertiveness of an Eight but struggle with staying power because the conflict that energizes Eights does not sustain Nines, who cannot escape their intuitive ability to see both sides in conflict. Nines with Eight wings frequently overcommit themselves, saying yes to a variety of added social engagements and work responsibilities that they do not have the energy to carry out when the deadline approaches.

My sister uses a Batman and Robin analogy to illustrate being a Nine with an Eight wing. She reflects that Batman embodies the Eight, leading the way to fight injustices everywhere. While Batman is at the helm, Robin (the Nine) is in sync with Batman every step of the way. As the "spicy" Nine with an Eight wing, my sister says that coworkers would think she is Batman most days. In truth, if Batman needed a day off, she could step in with ease. While her Eight wing equips her to don the cape without anyone knowing the difference, she cannot sustain a Batman existence because she is hardwired to be Robin.

Most Threes instinctively draw from a Two wing. Threes who have a Four wing are dealing with antithetical drives: the Three inclination to adjust themselves to fit the prescribed audience versus the Four inclination to loathe conformity, and the Three avoidance of emotional reflection versus the Four tendency to dive deep into emotional territory. A Four wing does not alter the motivational drive that Threes have to tailor themselves for success, but it does make it easier for these Threes to engage in solitude and introspection. Threes with Four wings are highly cognizant of their social battery, often identifying with core Five traits.

The second space worth acknowledging is contrasting Centers of Intelligence. The natural juxtaposition of feeling and thinking is visually represented through the placement of Four and Five at the base of the Enneagram. The largest space on the Enneagram is the span between feeling and thinking, or heart and head. In consideration of processing and support centers, nowhere on the Enneagram does feeling (subjective view) support thinking (objective reason) or thinking (objective reason) support feeling (subjective view).

Most Fives satisfy their inquisitive nature by staying in the Head Triad and leaning into their Six wing. Most Fours lean further into the Heart Triad, engaging the world with the help of their socially confident

Three wing. Fours with a Five wing and Fives with a Four wing bring a refreshingly unique gift to the world. Spanning the space between heart and head is a consistent challenge for most of us. Those who do so intuitively have the capacity to add measurable value to any organization.

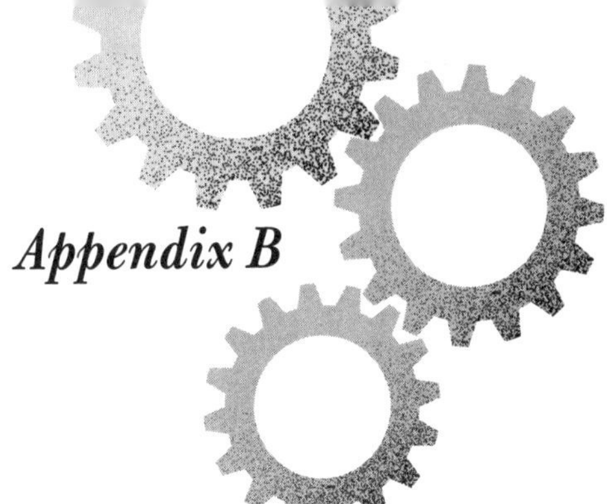

Appendix B

PART I REFLECTION QUESTIONS

1. We all have ingrained perceptions of what Doing, Feeling, and Thinking represent and how we utilize these centers in our daily lives. Take a moment to describe each center, as you view it, and provide examples of how you draw from each center at work and at home.
2. Explain the difference between objective thought and subjective thought. Provide an example of when you engage in each. Would you recategorize any examples that you provided in the first reflection question? (Did you list subjective thinking under Thinking instead of Feeling?)
3. Which of the three Centers of Intelligence are you most comfortable using? Why? Which of the three centers are you least comfortable using? Why?
4. Anger has long been linked to approach-oriented movement, or actions directed toward a target. How often do you feel anger? How do you use it to fuel action?
5. As human beings, we are all equipped with three Centers of Intelligence, but we do not draw from them in the same order or with the same frequency, often leading to disconnects at work. Think of a coworker with whom you struggle. Which Center of Intelligence do you believe they are using most? Is it different from the center you use most?

6. Take a moment to map the order that you draw from the Centers of Intelligence at work. Apply that mapping to your most recent performance review. Do you see a correlation between the center you use first or most and your identified strengths? Do you see a correlation between the center you use least or last and your identified areas for improvement?
7. Identify someone close to you who displays the following traits. What do you appreciate about this individual? In what ways are you similar to this individual? In what ways are you different?

   Members of the Independent (a.k.a. Aggressive) Stance:

   - have high self-confidence
   - tend to deflect personal questions
   - process quickly
   - think on their feet
   - have the most energy for action
   - are decisive
   - arc impatient with indecision and inaction
   - are oriented toward the future
8. Identify someone close to you who displays the following traits. What do you appreciate about this individual? In what ways are you similar to this individual? In what ways are you different?

   Members of the Responsive (a.k.a. Dependent) Stance:

   - feel strongly about doing well
   - like to make to-do lists
   - prefer to talk things through
   - ask the most questions
   - do not have strong personal boundaries
   - cannot ignore what is in front of them

- will take on more than what is theirs to do
- are oriented toward the present

9. Identify someone close to you who displays the following traits. What do you appreciate about this individual? In what ways are you similar to this individual? In what ways are you different?

   Members of the Solitary (a.k.a. Withdrawing) Stance:

   - can be difficult to read
   - do not like being told what to do
   - prefer to listen
   - have the least energy for action
   - rarely offer input without being asked
   - are comfortable being quiet observers
   - do not want to be the center of attention
   - are oriented toward the past